MASSACHUSETTS INSTITUTE OF TECHNOLOGY

1861-1961: A Hundred Year Chronicle

SCHOOL OF ARCHITECTURE AND PLANNING

by Caroline Shillaber

Acknowledgement is made to

Pietro Belluschi for his deep concern in presenting a historical record of the School;

Walter A. Netsch, Jr., for graciously consenting to support its publication;

Lawrence B. Anderson for prudently assisting in selecting the illustrations; and

Ralph Coburn for thoughtfully designing the book.

To look back at the record of our School's birth and growth seems particularly appropriate at the close of this one hundredth anniversary year. The historical continuity of events, the earnestness and wisdom of our forefathers in searching for native expressions, and their pervading sense of optimism, appear in concise form in this chronicle.

The prestige which the Institute enjoys today in America and abroad gives particular importance to this history. We are the oldest school of architecture in the United States. To learn of the peculiar faith of our fathers enables us to understand the full meaning of the changes that have occurred and are still occurring in our society. It gives us the insight to forge new tools for the future.

It is difficult to believe that at the time of the Civil War there was no formal instruction in architecture. The story of our School is indeed the story of architectural education in America—a continuing, never ending task.

Pietro Belluschi, Dean
School of Architecture and Planning

The young man who aspired to be an architect in Colonial America could choose between apprenticeship or studying abroad. Apprenticeship was a slow and uneven method of instruction depending entirely upon the aptitude of the pupil and the whim of a master builder or master carpenter; study abroad meant training at the Académie d'Architecture in Paris, a luxury which few, if any, Colonial architects experienced. The design of buildings was largely left to the master carpenters, who at first modeled their structures on "builders' guides" or on tradition, and later on "house pattern books." As the country developed, the need for trained architects became more apparent and more urgent.

One of the first Americans to recognize the need for systematic instruction in architecture was Thomas Jefferson. Master of many crafts, Jefferson was a skillful and inventive architect as proven in Monticello, the home that he designed for himself in Virginia. Education was one of his foremost concerns, and in 1814 he proposed to found a university which was to include architectural studies in its program of courses. When Jefferson's University of Virginia was founded, however, the introduction of an architecture curriculum was delayed for many years.

Meanwhile, William Barton Rogers, a young geologist who was teaching "natural philosophy" at the University, was formulating plans for a polytechnic school that would include an organized curriculum for teaching architecture. "Among practical pursuits," Rogers wrote in 1846, "there are perhaps none whose dependence upon the determinations of physical science is more generally recognized than those of the machinist, the engineer and the architect."[1]

In 1853 Rogers moved from Virginia to Boston, where he worked diligently to interest citizens in his plans for launching a school. His ideas were realized in 1861, when the Massachusetts General Court granted him a charter to found the Massachusetts Institute of Technology. The Civil War intervened, and the Institute opened for classes four years later, in 1865, with William Barton Rogers as its president.

Persevering in his ambition to add to the curriculum a course of study in the art of building, Rogers discussed the matter at length with a Boston architect, William Robert Ware.[2] A letter from Ware written in April, 1865, to the Secretary *pro tem* of the Institute, John D. Runkle, supported Rogers' proposals:

Let me say in the first place that next to a School of Mining a school of architecture seems to me just the thing for you to take up. It is eminently adapted to the wants of the community and to the resources of the School. There is not now in the country any adequate instruction in Construction and in Design none whatever, while the demand for skilled draughtsmen and competent architects is rapidly increasing in every part of the country.[3]

M.I.T.'s first professor of architecture, appointed in the fall of 1865, was William Robert Ware himself. By education and experience Ware was well prepared to devise a program of study. He was a graduate of Harvard College, Class of 1852, and of the Lawrence Scientific School at Harvard, and for a short period had studied and worked in New York in the office of Richard Morris Hunt. Hunt, the first American to graduate from the famous Ecole des Beaux-Arts in Paris, had returned from France to open a small *atelier* for young architects, hoping to infuse them with the same aspirations as their French contemporaries.[4] After leaving New York, Ware came to Boston in 1860, where he formed a partnership with Henry Van Brunt. The work of their firm included the First Church of Boston at the corner of Marlborough and Berkeley streets; the former Union Station in Worcester; the Episcopal Theological School in Cambridge; and for Harvard University, Weld Hall, Memorial Hall, and Gore Hall (no longer in existence). Ware was a member of the American Institute of Architects, founded in 1857, and was later made a Fellow.

William Ware was very conscious of the acute need for architectural education and in fact had personally assumed the responsibility for training young apprentices who worked in his office. In the previously quoted letter to Runkle, he referred to the profession as being in a "very inchoate and amorphous condition" and as failing "to make the most of the learning & ability which are at all times engaged in it."[5] His statement was no exaggeration. The Civil War was drawing to a close, and the country was entering a period of economic expansion. Industrial progress was changing both the methods and the materials of building. Iron, steel, and concrete were coming into use. New types of buildings were required: mills, railroad stations, factories for heavy industry, and office buildings with elevators. An efflorescence of exotic fashion in building had succeeded the dignified style of the Early Republic, and dwelling houses and public buildings were constructed with little relevance to function or taste.

Conditions at the time were described by Ware in a lecture to the Royal Institute of British Architects:[6]

Up to a very recent period—indeed I may say up to this time—the condition of architecture in the United States was very similar to that which it held in England twenty or thirty years ago, previous to the establishment of this Institute or of the architectural periodicals which have done so much for its improvement. Building, in general, was to a small extent only in the hands of professional architects and was, for the most part, carried on by builders and contractors. The professional architects of most of the large cities of the United States might be counted on the fingers of one hand, and their works were almost entirely confined to the more important public buildings, such as state houses, churches, custom-houses, and banks, the great bulk of the general work being done by masons, carpenters, and contractors of one sort and another, in which the interests of art were left to take care of themselves. In the last century this state of things perhaps did not do so much harm. At that time the respectable practice obtained of following the Rules of Vignola, and the consequence was, though there were no architects engaged in the work, the carpenters and mechanics following those rules covered the country with houses, not very novel indeed, but comely and decent. Amongst the photographs

6

The dwelling of a squire it might have been; it was the recreation hall of architecture students at M.I.T.

on the wall will be found illustrations of the works that were done under that regime—cubicle buildings with classical cornices and details, a repetition in wood of the sort of buildings erected in England during the last century, monuments of what the song calls the "good old colony times when we lived under the king"; these were the dwellings of the squires and local aristocracy, and the smaller houses were, in their degree, like unto them. The neighborhoods around Boston are full of them, dating from before the American Revolution, and some have attached to them a good deal of historical and local interest. One of the best of these old houses, of more than ordinary pretensions, is standing on the outskirts of Cambridge, being the house which was occupied by General Washington during the Siege of Boston and now acquiring a new title to fame as the residence of the poet Longfellow.

This state of things has long been overthrown, and a succession of styles has since prevailed, faint adumbrations of the phenomena which European architecture has meantime exhibited. The influence of Stuart and Revett, and of Pugin, of the Italian School, of the German School, and of the French School, of the rage for cottages, and of the rage for castles, may easily be traced, together with any number of styles which native enterprise has concocted out of these various elements, making the confusion worse by confounding everything. This enterprise would have lacked its most obvious and characteristic manifestation, and the chaos would have remained incomplete, if its agents had not everywhere assumed the title and degree of architect. Under this dispensation the rules of professional procedure became corrupted and lost, artistic work pretty much unknown, and even the traditions of professional etiquette and the old-fashioned way of doing business, so far as we had ever inherited them from the mother country, fell into abeyance and were forgotten. Such changes were of course natural to a society which, from being part of an old nation, had come to be a part of a new one; they were the phenomena of a state of transition, of which other things as well as the arts of building felt the influence.

In the Middle Ages building was a craft; "architects" were not known by that name until the Renaissance. A master builder, like Villard de Honnecourt in the thirteenth century, would make drawings for buildings[7] with no dimensions indicated, such matters being executed according to tradition handed down by apprenticeship from craftsman to craftsman. The system had tangible success in the magnificent Romanesque and Gothic buildings, handsome in their proportions, their stonework, their carvings, and their stained glass.

In the Renaissance, the builder became architect, educated in the grand manner of the age. He studied ancient authors, translating and writing commentaries on their works.[8] He published engravings[9]; he wrote books himself[10]; he became "architect," and was no longer known as a *"devisseur des bâtiments."* In the words of Jean Goujon, an architect of the sixteenth century must possess *"un bon entendement."* Appointed to design a building, he could not only draw plans and supervise workmen with technical competence but could also control the exchequer.

Organizations for formal instruction began to appear as early as the sixteenth century, when artists and architects banded together to form academies. In France the education of architects gained state support in 1671 with the founding of the Académie d'Architecture, which emerged two hundred years later, after several transmutations, as the Ecole des Beaux-Arts. Admission to the Ecole was by examination, and competition was carried to a high pitch in the last courses of design with the contest for the *Grand Prix,* which meant four years of additional study in Rome. While at the Ecole, students attached themselves at will to *ateliers.* These were small groups presided over by a *patron* or practicing architect, often of eminence, who criticized the work as it progressed. While the personality of the *patron* could engender a desire to excel, there was no integrated course of study.

In England, the counterpart of the European training by apprenticeship was a pupilage system. For a nominal fee paid to a practicing architect, students learned what they could through occasional instruction and office routine.

8

Education, however, was so uneven that towards the middle of the nineteenth century colleges offered courses to supplement pupilage training. One purpose of the Architectural Association, established in London in 1847, was to provide a system of study based on regular meetings for mutual discussion and criticism of designs. In other countries of Europe, the study of architecture was linked to instruction in polytechnic schools, as in the Technische Hochschulen in Germany, or to academies of art, such as Det Kongelige Kunst Akademi in Copenhagen.

William Ware's association with Hunt, a successful product of French training, inevitably led him to turn to the Ecole des Beaux-Arts in developing a system of architectural education at M.I.T. The resulting scheme showed the influence of the Ecole together with some considerable modifications. The *atelier* could not be copied in its French form, as American architects did not view their responsibilities toward education as idealistically as did their counterparts in France, who freely devoted time to criticism of Ecole work. However, certain elements of the French system did prevail. For example, the importance of design based on historical styles was emphasized. Competition was introduced through exhibition of student presentations, and judgment, when possible, was by juries composed of members of the staff who had not been previously concerned with the assigned problems. At M.I.T., the education in architecture differed from the Ecole chiefly in a planned curriculum with scheduled classes, including courses in construction, and in Ware's insistence on the need for a broad and general background not only of the history of architecture but of the entire realm of fine arts. Ware's *Outline* for the course of study that he proposed to establish, published in 1866,[11] set high standards of scholarship in the liberal arts. Ware felt that the study of ancient buildings as expressions of the ages which produced them was an essential background for designing modern buildings. Instruction was planned to embrace the scientific study of construction and materials, while the theory and practice of design was to be learned by the study of historic examples.

Later Ware wrote:

In the performance of this work we propose to do nothing that can be dispensed with, leaving matters that can be learned in offices to be learned there, and not encumbering the student with useless and irrelevant lore. At the same time we recognize the fact that many practical matters whose details may best be learned by office work need a systematic and theoretical discussion for their proper comprehension, and this discussion we propose to afford.[12]

In his correspondence with William Barton Rogers, Ware had written that he should not consider himself "competent to undertake any great part either in the organization of the school or its administration without the aid of a special preparation,"[13] by which he meant personal observation of existing instruction in Europe. Accordingly, funds were supplied partly by M.I.T. and partly by private sources for Ware to visit England, Scotland, France, Italy, and the Low Countries, and to purchase books, casts, models, and drawings. So many of Ware's friends in Milton contributed to the total sum, which amounted to $5,000, that it was called the Milton Scholarship Fund.

Ware traveled widely and questioned diligently. He visited collections representing art in all its forms, noting especially casts, models, and photographs. To these, he believed, should be added a library: "A well-selected though not necessarily a very large library, so placed as to be easily used in connection with these collections, and portfolios of first-rate architectural drawings, would be invaluable."[14] He returned with purchases, supplemented by numerous gifts, that included books and papers, 2,000 photographs, 500 prints, 400 plaster casts, 200 crayon drawings, 40 water colors, architectural drawings, tiles, pottery, and stained glass. The books and drawings formed the nucleus of the library that he had envisioned. It was Ware's custom to grant one student in architecture the cost of his tuition in return for "taking care of the library and other properties, and doing such work as he can for the

10

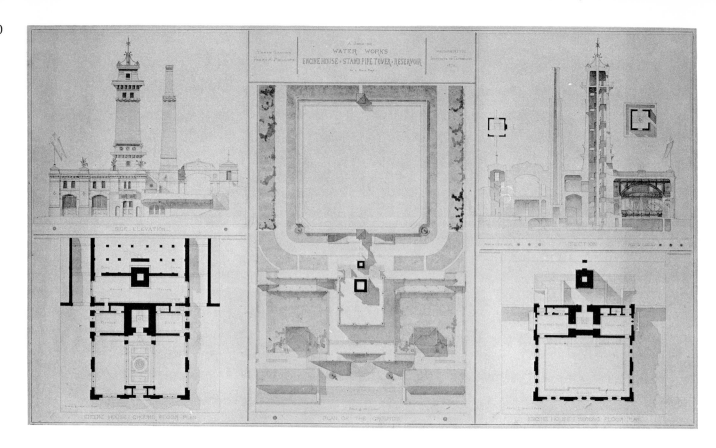

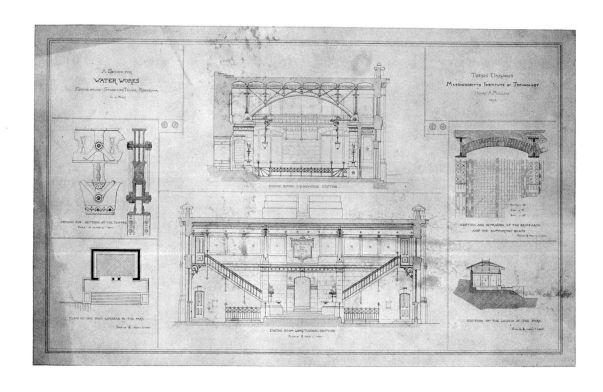

A Design for Water Works, Engine House, Stand Pipe Tower, and Reservoir in a Public Park, by Henry A. Phillips, was the first thesis awarded the M.I.T. degree of Bachelor of Science in Architecture (1873). The drawings epitomize nineteenth century taste in their delicate rendering in pencil, India ink, and water color "tinting." The plan that includes two loggias expresses the leisure of the age.

instructors."[15] The miscellaneous objects were arranged in an architectural museum.

The Department of Architecture opened in October, 1868, with classes held in the Rogers Building on Boylston Street, Boston, which was M.I.T.'s home until 1916. There were four students enrolled in the regular four-year course leading to the Bachelor of Science in Architecture. In addition to instruction in mathematics and engineering required of all students, courses were offered in architectural design, ornament and details, architectural drawing, perspective, and specifications, and there were lectures on history and the orders. This was the beginning of a curriculum founded on Ware's belief that it was "the object of the department to give the instruction that cannot be obtained in architects' offices, leaving students to learn what can there best be learned during the term of their service as draughtsmen."[16] The Institute also offered a special two-year professional course to pupils from architects' offices, twelve of whom were enrolled in the Department's first year. This two-year course was discontinued after 1890, although the Institute continued to admit special students.

Enrollment in the Department increased in the following year to ten full-time students and twelve from local offices. Francis W. Chandler, who had worked as a student in the Ware and Van Brunt office and studied in the Atelier Daument in Paris, was added to the staff to teach design, and two instructors were appointed for water color and crayon. The Boston Society of Architects offered two prizes. Ware wrote in his annual report for the year that much of the class work was in the Gothic style.

Chandler stayed only from October to the following April. To succeed him, Ware chose a student from the Première Classe at the Ecole des Beaux-Arts, Eugène Létang (1842-1892), who came to the Institute in 1871.[17] For the remaining years of his life Létang taught design as derived from classic sources. Possessed of a passion for meticulous draftsmanship, he sought throughout the years of his teaching to inspire his students with high standards of drawing as well as reverence for ancient styles of architecture. Létang was associated with Henry H. Richardson when he

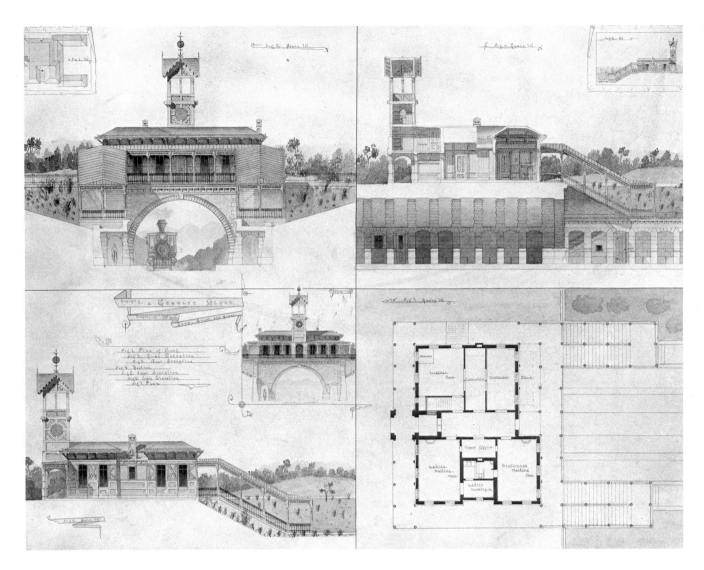

Design for a Country Depot Employing Wood, Iron, Brick, and Stone, by William B. Dowse, 1871, was a typical Gothic quotation of a school problem popular for the next hundred years.

14

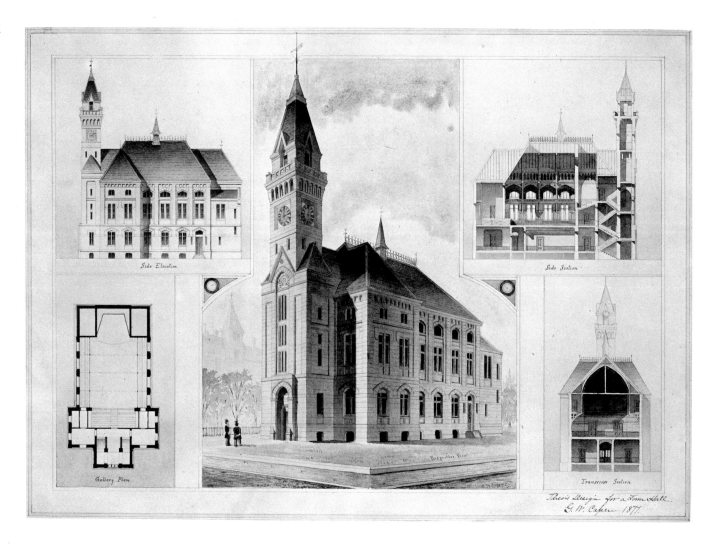

Few New England towns do not boast a town hall, school, or library in the manner of George W. Capen's Thesis Design for a Town Hall in 1877. It was projected for a town and a society that today are difficult to recall. Lighting by gas was more common than by electricity, the telephone was scarcely a year old, and iron construction was undergoing rapid experimentation in New York and Chicago.

was designing the State House in Albany, New York, and he also submitted designs for the Boston Public Library.

Shortly after the establishment of the Department of Architecture, the Rogers Building served as headquarters for the fifth annual (1871) convention of the American Institute of Architects. "Education of the young" was now of primary concern to the profession, and its Committee on Education was led by Ware as chairman. The A.I.A. encouraged young students by donating prizes for scholastic achievement.

The Class of 1873 was the first to include a representative of the Department among the graduates. Henry A. Phillips, the first to complete the course, did not choose a career in architecture, but he always retained a lively interest in the progress of the Department.

In his Annual Report for the year 1873, President John D. Runkle, reviewing the progress of the Department of Architecture, pointed out that the Department began with "neither written nor traditional precedents to serve as guides in the instruction, nor were there any suitable collections for illustration.[18] We are happy to say," he continued, "that this early and not entirely satisfactory phase of the department is gradually, but surely, passing away. Regular students of thorough preparation and recognized ability are beginning to enroll themselves."[19]

As President Runkle implied, textbooks were totally lacking; many of the early teachers therefore wrote treatises on their favorite subjects. Ware wrote two books and compiled a series of illustrations on the orders, but none was published until after he left M.I.T.[20]

As early as 1875 the few courses were expanded into a curriculum, starting in the second year with drawing, history, and design; continuing in the third year with design, theory, drawing, specifications, and stereotomy; and culminating in the fourth year with design, architectural ornament and detail, specifications, drawing, stability and strength of structures, and building materials. In 1878, the course of study was enlarged. Architectural history was divided into periods and became four courses. Sketching was a requirement each year. Additional subjects included decorative arts, masonry, plumbing, bridges and roofs,

16

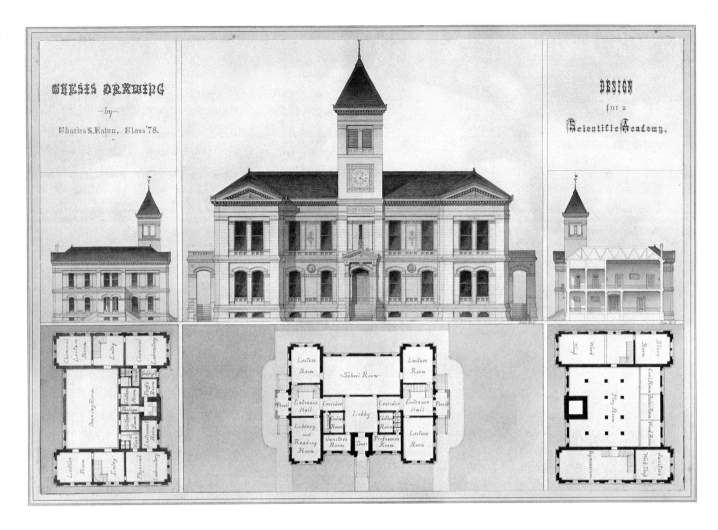

Design for a Scientific Academy, by Charles S. Eaton, was drawn in 1878. In the preceding year, *The American Architect and Building News* had concluded a two-year series of articles on architectural students; the second of which, urging young men to go to a professional school, rather than trusting to what they could learn in an architect's office, reported that

The standard of respectable professional attainment is much higher than it was a few years ago, and it requires

much more effort to attain it.

In stressing the importance of good draftmanship, the fifth article recommended that the student store his mind with forms in order to discipline his sense of proportion and composition:

Every style will furnish him abundance of material; and in this eclectic age he is compelled, or at least strongly impelled, to collect his material from all sides, to make himself acquainted more or less with the whole range of architectural precedent.

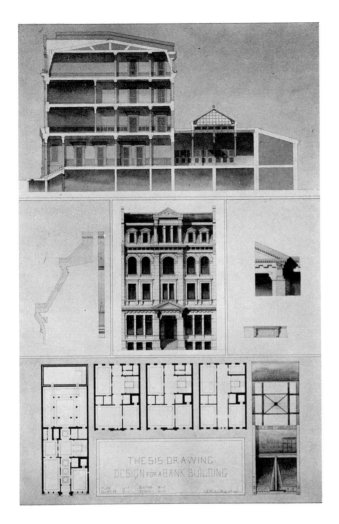

A Bank Building by Charles M. Wilkes, 1881, expressed devotion to ancient Greece through its pediments.

carpentry, shop work, and style and composition—a title which should have given flair to dull imagination.

The year 1876 saw the Department's staff and students, joined by a dozen alumni, encamped for a fortnight on the grounds of the University of Pennsylvania while taking part in the International Exposition in Philadelphia. Drawings exhibited by both students and alumni attracted favorable attention, especially from visitors from abroad. A gift of casts exhibited in the Spanish Pavilion and drawings made in the schools of Madrid was donated to the Department at the close of the Exposition. Gifts of books from London and Paris, as well as from donors in this country, continued to augment the volumes in the library.

Ware resigned from the Institute in 1881, when he was invited to establish a school of architecture at Columbia University. His span of office at M.I.T.—1868 to 1881—coincided with an era of progress in the development of architecture as a profession in this country. During this period three universities besides M.I.T. had begun to give instruction in architecture: Illinois in 1868, Cornell in 1871, and Syracuse in 1873. The first American periodical devoted wholly to architecture, *The American Architect and Building News,* was published in Boston in 1876. In 1870 the United States Census listed over 2,000 architects, and there was an increase of more than 1,300 in the next decade.

An age of elegant building had arrived. The city of Boston, already rich in Greek Revival, was gradually assuming an urbane appearance with fine residential sections and distinguished public buildings of Victorian Gothic and Renaissance styles. From Arlington Street Church (1859), rows of town houses extended from the newly laid-out Public Garden. Ware and Van Brunt's First Church (1865-1867) and Richard Upjohn's Congregational Church (1866) introduced the Gothic styles to the city, while William G. Preston's building for M.I.T. (1866) and his New England Museum of Natural History brought the flavor of French Renaissance. (A grander flourish of the French style was to be found in the commercial district, where the City Hall of Gridley James Fox Bryant had been built in 1862.) Copley Square—with H. H. Richardson's Trinity Church (1874-1877), the New Old South Church (Cummings and Sears, 1877), and the Museum of Fine Arts (first structure designed by Sturgis and Brigham, 1876)—reflected the good taste of its individual architects. Later, the Public Library of Stanford White's design (1887) added the final touch of dignity as its massive Renaissance lines balanced the Romanesque Trinity. Victorian Gothic made a flamboyant debut in Cambridge with the building of Memorial Hall (Ware and Van Brunt, 1878), a masterpiece that warmed the heart of a visiting Frenchman, who, indifferent to other buildings in the region, exclaimed that here was *"quelque chose!"*

Upon the resignation of Ware, Theodore M. Clark (1845-1909) became head of the Department. Clark had worked in H. H. Richardson's office for seven years and later had his own practice in Boston. He made three additions to the staff of the Department: William P. P. Longfellow, Ross Turner, and David Gregg, to teach perspective, water color, and rendering. Longfellow later compiled a textbook on perspective[21] and wrote other books on architectural history.[22] Turner published a small book on water color for beginners,[23] and Gregg's instruction on rendering in pen and ink was printed in small booklets.[24] Clark himself taught construction.[25] A course in heating and ventilation was introduced in 1882, and iron construction was first taught in 1883. Frank Eugene Kidder, later known for the numerous editions of his *Architects' Handbook,* attempted to inaugurate an architectural laboratory in which to illustrate the theory of construction by experiment and by testing materials, but the course had to be abandoned for lack of time in the curriculum. C. Howard Walker, a local architect whose early training had been partly at the Ecole des Beaux-Arts, began in 1884 a series of lectures on Philosophy of the Fine Arts, enriched by the facilities offered by the Museum of Fine Arts in Boston. Walker's lectures continued until 1899 and resumed from 1901 to 1933.

In 1883 the Department of Architecture made the first of many moves into the "new building" which had been erected on the corner of Boylston and Clarendon streets

The influence of H. H. Richardson appears in the thesis drawing for a Railway Station by John G. Eppendorff. The thesis was submitted in 1883, two years before the death of Richardson who was already the most heroic figure in the American architectural scene. Though a small building, the station is a primer of Richardson's more massive work in its solid appearance, textured walls, and repeated arches.

THESIS DRAWING
A RAILWAY STATION

20 The Paris Opéra, designed by J.-L.-C. Garnier, was the most sumptuous building in Paris after the New Louvre. For his Thesis Design for An Opera House, Eleazer B. Homer needed only to simplify the plan—a form of emulation that was taking place the world over wherever opera houses were being built.

THESIS.

Mass. Inst. Technology.

Design for a Theatre.

ELEAZER B. HOMER

May 10th. 1885.

Side Elevation.

SCALE ⅛ INCH = 1 FOOT.

22

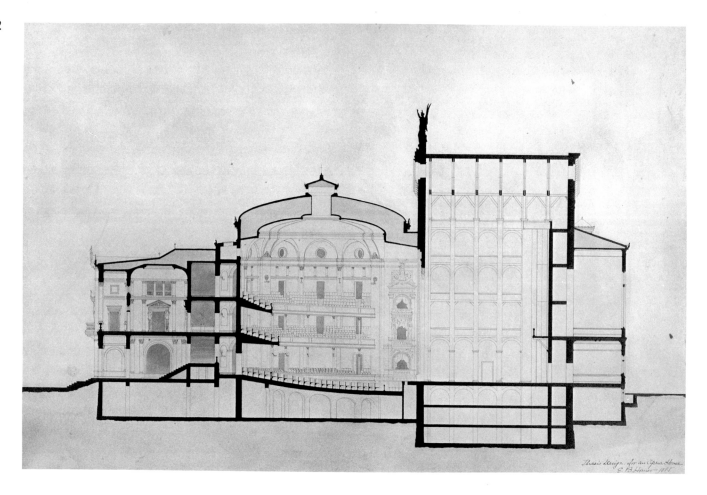

Neither Homer in his thesis
of 1885, nor any other architect, ever equalled the grand
flourish of the Opéra in Paris
that had been completed in
1875.

and which also housed the Departments of Chemistry and Physics.

At about this time M.I.T. began to benefit from the generosity of Arthur Rotch. Like other practicing architects in Boston, Rotch gave occasional lectures to the Department of Architecture; he was also a member of the M.I.T. Corporation. He had graduated from Harvard in 1871 and studied briefly at M.I.T before entering the office of Henry Van Brunt; later he studied at the Ecole des Beaux-Arts and then joined partnership to practice architecture with George T. Tilden.

While in Europe, Rotch had traveled extensively, an opportunity which he found extremely rewarding. In 1883, together with other members of his family, he established the Rotch Traveling Scholarship,[26] which enabled a student of architecture to travel for a year or more in Europe. The Scholarship, not restricted to any one college, was placed in the hands of a committee of the Boston Society of Architects,[27] which still selects the recipient. The generosity of Arthur Rotch was not limited to the Institute but extended to the newly founded Department of Architecture at Harvard, and both departments benefited at his death by large bequests. M.I.T. gave his name to its library which became, officially, the Arthur Rotch Memorial Library of Architecture.

In the early years there were other young men who studied for a year or two at M.I.T. and later became leading architects of their day. One of these was Christopher Grant La Farge, who won the competition for the Cathedral of St. John the Divine in New York City, although his Romanesque design enjoyed only brief triumph over the Gothic that later prevailed. While the Cathedral was the chief project of his lifetime, La Farge was a prolific designer of ecclesiastical architecture.

The Greene brothers, Henry M. and Charles S., attended M.I.T. before going to California, where the brothers' work is receiving belated recognition. Heralding an indigenous style of domestic architecture, the Greenes developed a wholly individual bungalow style in which they used materials and details in a craftsmanlike way. Louis Sullivan began

A Railway Station by William L. Brainerd, 1886, shows the rather romantic tower which characterized such structures in the latter half of the nineteenth century.

his study of architecture at M.I.T. at the age of sixteen. Finding formal education incompatible with his emerging theories, he left after one year (1872-1873), tried other schools, and eventually found his way to Chicago. Sullivan's fierce approach to his career achieved individuality in an eclectic age.

Year by year, enrollment in the Department gradually increased. The five years between 1886 and 1891 brought the number of students from thirteen to thirty-three. When but thirteen students were registered in the Department, twelve of them, with the *esprit de corps* peculiar to early schools of architecture the world over, organized the Architectural Society, which later produced and published an interesting review. Towards the close of the decade, in 1888, Theodore M. Clark resigned to become editor of *The American Architect and Building News*.

Francis Ward Chandler, who returned as head of the Department, brought an era of progress and development. Paris-trained at the Ecole des Beaux-Arts, he had also studied with Ware and Van Brunt in their Boston office. Chandler had assisted Ware at M.I.T. in the academic year of 1869-1870; since then he had been Assistant Supervising Architect of the Treasury Department in Washington and had also been associated with Edward C. Cabot in the architectural firm of Cabot and Chandler. He was a member of the Boston Art Commission, an honorary member of the American Institute of Architects, and a director of the American Academy in Rome. For a number of years Chandler served as architectural advisor to the mayor of Boston.

Chandler revised the four-year course and later was able to establish a year of graduate study. Iron and steel construction was made an important course, and courses were added in acoustics, sanitary science, the history of construction, and history of art. Two M.I.T. graduates joined the teaching staff; Eleazer B. Homer in 1887 and Walter H. Kilham in 1889. Both opened independent offices in Boston, although Homer transferred his practice to Providence after he was appointed Director of the Rhode

THESIS

MASS INST TECHNOLOGY

MAY 10 1886

DESIGN

ELEVATED RAILWAY STATION

W. L. BRAINERD

BROOKLINE AVENUE ELEVATION

SCALE 1/8 INCH=ONE FOOT

Island School of Design. Kilham, a winner of the Rotch Traveling Scholarship, resigned in 1901 but remained in Boston as co-founder of Kilham, Hopkins, and Greeley.

At this time there were references to a five-year course in architecture, though actually this was the four-year course taken at a slower pace. Chandler also attempted to strengthen the two-year course with a view to attracting older students, but results were not wholly satisfactory and the course was discontinued. In order to put the long summer months of vacation to practical use, Chandler requested that students not engaged actively in architects' offices spend part of the summer on specified problems, a project to which they responded with enthusiasm. By 1891 President Walker was able to report that "the growing success of this—always first-rate—department constitutes one of the most striking features of the Institute."[28]

A booklet describing Course IV, the curriculum in Architecture, published in 1890,[29] indicates Chandler's adherence to Ware's belief in a broad and general education for architects:

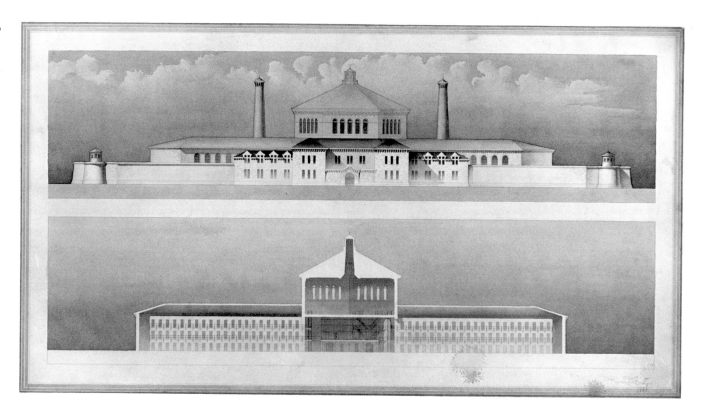

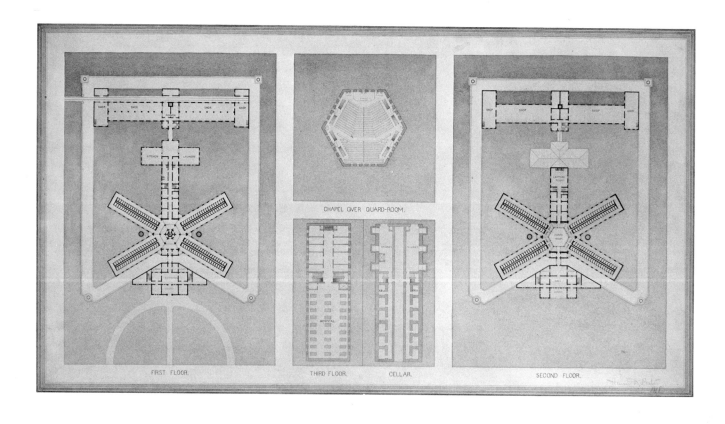

CHAPEL OVER QUARD-ROOM.

FIRST FLOOR.   THIRD FLOOR.   CELLAR.   SECOND FLOOR.

The plan for a Penitentiary by Henry D. Bates, 1888, is similar to the layout devised by John Haviland in 1829 for the Eastern State Penitentiary in Philadelphia, the first built in the United States. Blocks of cells radiating from a central rotunda that served as guard room provided solitude and segregation for every inmate from his neighbors. While not an ideal solution, the scheme represented an early step in the progress of penal institutions.

The studies and exercises of the course in Architecture have been carefully selected and arranged, that those who graduate shall be liberally educated and shall possess a thorough professional training. During the entire course, therefore, studies have been introduced which are directed toward the student's mental development and his knowledge of letters, language, politics, and history.

The importance of construction was emphasized:

In the strictly professional work, great stress is laid upon the student's acquisition and mastery of the principles that underlie sound construction. To the work in the draughting room and in the laboratory of applied mechanics is added the examination of buildings actually in course of construction, to enable the student intelligently to deal with problems in architectural practice.[30]

And good design was still derived from ancient monuments:

The cultivation of the student's taste in color and in form is accomplished by the solution of varied problems in the art of design, by the study of the history of architecture and the history of ornament, and by practice in water-color and freehand drawing.[31]

In 1892 the Department made its second move, this time into the newly built Architectural Building, designed by Chandler, on the corner of Stuart and Clarendon streets. There were five stories, with a basement for building appliances, a laboratory for testing materials, and a complete plumbing plant for a small dwelling house. The library now included 800 volumes and 10,000 photographs and merited a catalogue which was printed by the Institute.[32]

Eugène Létang died in 1892. His influence is revealed unmistakably in the three volumes of the *Technology Architectural Review*[33] published by students in the Department. The *Review* consisted of plans and renderings of school problems, with criticism by Létang and articles by

Henry Van Brunt and other lecturers. The formality of plan and beauty of draftsmanship of the students' work reproduced in the *Review* reveal Létang's life-long devotion to the classic style. While he had not transplanted the *atelier* system from the Ecole des Beaux-Arts, he had brought from Paris the competitive spirit in posting and judging completed designs. Juries often included practicing architects in Boston; and, as in Paris, noted architects not of the student's own *atelier* criticized his work, determined promotion, and awarded prizes.

Chandler, as Ware before him, turned to Paris for Létang's successor, whom he found in Désiré Despradelle. Born in 1862, Despradelle had been a brilliant student at the Ecole des Beaux-Arts which he entered at the age of twenty, first among 140 candidates. For seven years he studied in the *atelier* of J.-L. Pascal, winning many prizes; later he was appointed collaborator on Public Buildings and National Palaces in France. Despradelle came to the Institute in 1893 where his mode of instruction was an immediate success. A brilliant designer himself, with a "facile black pencil," Despradelle was concerned primarily with developing a talent in his students for evolving good proportions for their buildings and correct scale in their structures. He was successful in many competitions, receiving one of the first awards in the International Phoebe Hearst Competition for the University of California; later he was appointed to the Board of Advisers for the University. Despradelle served in an advisory capacity to architects for several buildings, and as partner of Stephen Codman he shared in a number of commercial building projects. One of the Codman and Despradelle designs may still be seen in the Berkeley Building[34] on Boylston Street, Boston. Another is the Peter Bent Brigham Hospital, a commission won in competition. The French government purchased two of Despradelle's drawings for a Beacon of Progress, a towering concept for a monument to arise on the site of the World's Fair of 1893 in Chicago. The renderings, with planes advancing and receding, were in themselves striking examples of French imagination.

Despradelle's years at the Institute began auspiciously

A Quarantine Hospital by Arthur V. Edwards, 1889, is a Beaux-Arts design for a utilitarian structure. Its spaciousness, courts, towers, and miniature lighthouses ignored the medical profession's growing pleas for practical, rather than monumental, hospitals.

THESIS DESIGN • A QVARANTINE HOSPITAL • A·V·EDWARDS·1889

THESIS DRAWING – A MVSEVM OF NATVRAL HISTORY – M.I.T. 1889 – 1:16 SCALE.

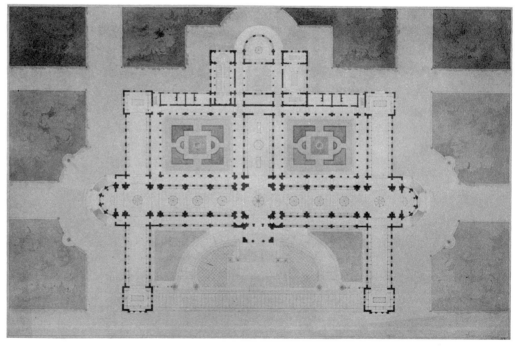

When Walter H. Kilham was drawing this thesis, A Museum of Natural History, 1889, with an iron roof truss, innovations in building techniques were making it outmoded. Electricity was a new force to be reckoned with for its practical and esthetic application. The steel frame was replacing iron construction, and the vast potential of reinforced concrete was being tentatively explored. It was an era of progress and achievement in every phase of the building industry.

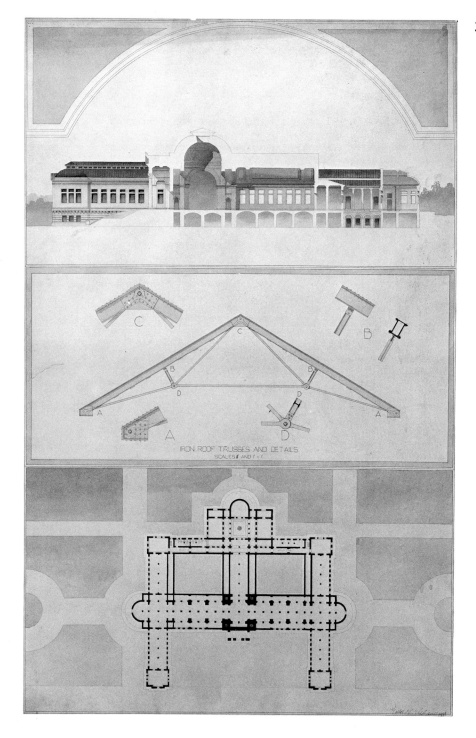

with the largest enrollment in the history of the course, fifty regular students and sixty-nine special students including twenty-three college graduates. There were seven students in the graduate course which had been organized on a one-year basis, although only one of the students graduated in June. Samuel W. Mead, who had been teaching since 1893, assisted Despradelle in design until 1914. Mead had been the second winner of the Rotch Traveling Scholarship. Allen H. Cox '98 was added to the design staff in 1903 and remained until 1912. Both men were engaged in architectural practice, Mead as a member of the Cabot, Everett, and Mead firm (later, Everett and Mead). Cox had studied at the Ecole des Beaux-Arts.

Chandler wrote in his Annual Report for 1893 that he had striven "to build up a class of students who, having completed all the undergraduate work, can give at least an entire additional year to design."[35] When, in the following year, a few of the graduate students returned for still another year of study, Chandler explained the trend of the Department:

The department is aiming to show that a post-graduate course of two years, continuing the same scheme of studies, governed by the same traditions, is of greater value to the student than to split the course by spending part of the time here and part abroad at the foreign schools. School training in the strictly professional work should teach in the highest degree the principles of composition, balance, proportion, and scale. To accomplish this requires years of hard and uninterrupted study, under instruction of unquestioned ability. Then comes the time for a year or more of foreign travel, when the value of the previous training will be apparent in the greater appreciation of historical architecture.[36]

The first M.I.T. summer school in architecture was held in Chicago in 1893, since the World's Fair was thought to offer "an exceptional opportunity for comparative study of both foreign and domestic art and construction,"[37] but no mention was made of the structural inventiveness that was introducing new methods of building. Perhaps, al-

The sophistication of the French Renaissance gave a borrowed air of elegance to urban houses as well as to great country houses of the Nineties. Frederick M. Mann's Club, submitted as his thesis in 1894, was intended for men of wealth and distinction in an age dominated by European taste and precedent. It would not have been out of place among the mansions and clubs on New York's Fifth Avenue.

though official records are silent, the class did see the Monadnock Building by Daniel H. Burnham, the Home Insurance Building of William Le Baron Jenney, and the Auditorium of Louis Sullivan. The latter architect, when he studied in the M.I.T. Department in 1872, found it "but a pale reflection of the Ecole des Beaux-Arts" presided over by Ware, a gentleman of moderate attainments, and his assistant, Eugène Létang, of sallow earnestness. The young Louis did concede that he "had gone at his studies faithfully enough. He learned not only to draw, but to draw very well."[38] Louis spent enough time in the library to become acquainted with styles which he found were human in contrast to the orders, which he described as "fairy tales of the long ago."[39]

The summer schools, initiated with the trip to Chicago, continued the following year in Salem, Massachusetts, with classes making measured drawings of colonial buildings in towns along the coast. In 1896 the school consisted of a bicycle trip by twenty students in England and France. For seventy-six days, with sketchbooks and cameras, they dutifully recorded historic styles of the past, from Romanesque to Renaissance. Eleazer B. Homer, faculty member in charge of the pilgrimage, remarked that only the bicycles suffered accidents in Europe. Leisurely junkets in Europe, with sketchbook and knapsack, were enjoyed thereafter for many years. A detailed report was written by Homer for the *Technology Quarterly* of March, 1897. The young men returned to America with intensified devotion to Greek, Roman, Gothic, and Renaissance styles.

M.I.T. had admitted women students in 1883, and two years later the Department of Architecture admitted a woman to its ranks. The first to graduate was Sophia Hayden of the Class of 1890, who won a competition for the design of the Women's Building at the World's Fair of 1893 in Chicago.

Russell W. Porter was following the accepted trend in French classical for his Governor's House in a State Capitol, 1896, that appears on the following pages. It was the style of Newport, of Philadelphia, of Fifth Avenue mansions. It was the country house, the urban house, the club. Whether it was French Renaissance or French provincial, it was a mark of wealth and social distinction. Its most extravagant and lavish expression was in Vanderbilt's Biltmore in Asheville, North Carolina, which had been modeled on three French chateaux. The style flourished, then disappeared —except for minor imitations in suburban dwellings—without contributing to or influencing the course of American architecture.

Porter's mansion was French Renaissance, embellished with decoration and set in gardens of the same scale. It was an urbane building exactly on a main axis in an ample setting of gardens, terraces, fountains, and monumental gateways.

38 Choir Stall by William T. Aldrich, 1902. The Gothic Revival was the preferred style for churches when richness of effect and perfection of detail appealed to a congregation. Ruskin's crusade, begun in the middle of the nineteenth century with the publication of *The Seven Lamps of Architecture* and carried on through reprinting of his books until 1900, had triumphed in the United States through the works of Ralph Adams Cram, Bertram Grosvenor Goodhue, and Richard Upjohn. Cram, with numerous books and articles, had reinforced example with criticism that received avid interest in its day.

By the close of the nineteenth century eleven American colleges and universities were teaching architecture, including Cornell (1871), the University of Illinois[40] and Syracuse (1873), Columbia (1881), Pennsylvania (1890), and Harvard (1895). A Society of Beaux-Arts Architects, later to become the Beaux-Arts Institute of Design, had been formed in 1894 by enthusiastic alumni of the Ecole des Beaux-Arts in Paris, of whom there were more than a hundred in the United States, to perpetuate the principles of taste of the Ecole and to encourage American students to enter the school. Competitions open to students of the various American schools were sponsored. A Paris Prize (later renamed the Lloyd Warren Scholarship, in memory of its founder) was also donated entitling the winner to enter the Ecole with two years' expenses paid. M.I.T. students won one or more prizes each year; but while the spirit of competition was considered as beneficial here as at the Ecole, the time required to prepare drawings, taken out of time for class work, increased to such an extent that the Department later decided to withdraw.

Other prizes were made available annually by Arthur Rotch from a bequest left at his death in 1894. Long a benefactor of the Department and member of the Visiting Committee, he had given freely of his time and counsel.

The library was rapidly becoming a first-rate working library enriched by volumes, prints, photographs, and casts. Twenty-six thousand slides for lectures had been purchased as the nucleus of a collection which has now grown to include more than 50,000 slides of architecture, painting, and sculpture. Hundreds of books were donated, many of them of folio size and superbly illustrated. Architectural casts had become so numerous that they presented a problem in display and storage, although they were considered important accessories in teaching design. Photographs were mounted by the thousands for the time-honored custom of teaching architectural history by requiring students to memorize views of European buildings, a method that has not altered in schools all across the country from that day to this, despite improvements in graphic media.

Marion L. Mahony (later Mrs. Walter Burley Griffin), who graduated in 1894, was one of Frank Lloyd Wright's principal designers at The Studio in Oak Park, Illinois, for more than ten years. Her fine renderings, with hidden signature, appear in publications on the first cycle of Wright's work.

In 1898 the Department moved from its then cramped quarters into the Pierce Building on Trinity Place. Once again the move was to a building that had been designed by one of M.I.T.'s own professors, Eleazer B. Homer, in collaboration with other members of the Institute. Adequate space was provided for an exhibition room and a library with alcove plan that was adopted sixty years and two buildings later in its present quarters in Cambridge. Books and prints were accumulating for Professor Sumner's course in history. John O. Sumner, appointed in 1894, had gradually elaborated his course until it became an intensive study of ancient and medieval architecture, its evolution, qualities, and transition from one style to another.[41] He retired in 1933.

At this time two options were offered to third-year classes: Architectural Engineering, first in 1898; and Landscape Architecture, beginning in 1900. The demand for graduates trained in the principles of steel construction had forced the adoption of a course in structural design. New modes of building, different styles of architecture, and structures of a dimension formerly inconceivable were required for the industrial progress that was sweeping over the country. Later years and new materials inevitably caused changes and additions of courses in concrete and reinforced concrete. William Henry Lawrence, a member of the Class of 1891 who returned to teach in the same year, was in charge of the option in Architectural Engineering until it was discontinued in 1938. As aids to teaching, Lawrence published two books: *Elements of Shades and Shadows*[42] and *Principles of Architectural Perspective*,[43] which became a popular textbook and went through several editions.

With progress came prosperity in building and imitation of European grandeur on a colossal, but often tasteless, scale. The proprietors of industrial enterprises liked their houses big, imposing, and surrounded with parks and gardens containing all the elements of Renaissance elegance, if lacking similar charm. The second option, Landscape Architecture, was therefore begun optimistically in the spring of 1900. It was directed by Guy Lowell, a graduate of the Department of Architecture in 1894, who had designed a number of major buildings, including the Boston Museum of Fine Arts.

In his plans for houses, whether large or small, Lowell regarded the layout of the grounds as an integral part of the total design. His admiration for European gardens, especially Italian, resulted in two publications on Italian villas and strongly influenced his work in America, as can be seen in many of the elaborate compositions that he designed. His book, *American Gardens*,[44] shows the highly decorative style of garden design replete with terraces, pavilions, pools, and statuary that was characteristic of the early twentieth century.

Although no precedent existed for teaching landscape architecture, a curriculum was planned that included composition, grading, and field study in horticulture and botany at the Arnold Arboretum. In Brookline, long known for its many splendid gardens which dated from the middle of the nineteenth century, the owners opened their gates to class study. The option enjoyed only brief popularity, however, and was discontinued as an undergraduate course in 1904; it continued as a graduate course until 1909. By that time, Harvard was offering a well-organized course of study in landscape architecture. Lowell continued to give lectures for several years on a voluntary basis, his salary reverting to M.I.T. for fellowships.

The profession of landscape architecture, still in the early stages of its development, drew into its ranks men and women who had benefited from the brief program at M.I.T. Already it had attracted two members who had been at the Institute too early to take advantage of the curriculum in landscape architecture, Stephen Child '88 and Arthur A. Shurcliff '94, both pioneers in garden design and park planning. George E. Burnap, who graduated in

With sights set on the American Academy in Rome, where he later studied, it is not surprising that Edgar I. Williams should design an Italian Villa in 1908. Guy Lowell, an authority on Italian gardens, was teaching landscape architecture, and there were several magnificent examples of Italian design in the vicinity of Boston, notably Faulkner Farm in Brookline and H. H. Hunnewell's home in Wellesley.

the Landscape Architecture option in 1906, became a noted   43
park planner. For his work as government landscape architect in Washington he received a degree from the Ecole
des Hautes Etudes Urbaines, University of Paris. Two
women graduates, Marian C. Coffin '04 and Mabel K. Bab-
cock '08, were life-long practitioners of landscape architecture, which was evolving as an independent profession
in the early years of the twentieth century.

In 1900 the Institute was one of two American colleges
of engineering and architecture invited by the United
States Commission to show designs at the Paris Exposition,
and the French Government later asked the Institute to
present a number of the exhibited renderings to the Ecole
des Beaux-Arts. The renderings for the Beacon of Progress
by Despradelle, previously described, were also exhibited
and bought by France.[45] While Despradelle was still able
to evoke fine academic work from his students, there was
a growing attraction toward the option in Architectural
Engineering, which was earning a reputation among architects' offices. Instruction in this option included advanced
courses in applied mechanics and in theory of structures,
and practical problems in structural design.

The rapid changes that were altering old concepts of
construction at the beginning of the twentieth century had
given an impetus to the study of architecture. Over a hundred students were enrolled regularly in the Department.
With the outside world clamoring for architects, academic
training could no longer stop with the close of the Renaissance. Ware's plan of education had to be expanded to
include both the development of talent and the mastery of
building techniques. Urban expansion, industrial progress,
and the growth of suburbs required architects who could
not only furnish designs but could also apply theoretical
knowledge to new forms and new materials.

The Department, while broadening its scope to en-
compass technological progress, did not wholly lose sight
of its original aim, to teach that "architecture is essentially
a fine art," and that "its successful practice demands the
possession of a broad general cultivation, a liberal training
in design, and a thorough knowledge of the principles

underlying sound construction."[46] The Paris influence was still strong at M.I.T. as well as at other schools established during the early period of architectural education. That the courses at M.I.T. partook liberally of the spirit of the Ecole was recognized with singular distinction when Andrew Nicholas Rebori, a graduate of the Class of 1907, passed the first two competitions for the Paris Prize. Another graduate of 1907, Ernest F. Lewis, was admitted to the American Academy in Rome.[47] The Department had previously contributed a Director to the Academy, when Gorham P. Stevens '98 was chosen for that post in 1911.

By the end of the first decade of the twentieth century, changes in staff began to occur in rapid succession. Francis Chandler retired as head of the Department in 1911, and the Boston Society of Architects established in his name a prize fund to be awarded to students in the fifth-year class. After Chandler's retirement, the Department was in the charge of Désiré Despradelle for one academic year and of James Knox Taylor '79[48] for the two succeeding years, 1912 to 1914. Taylor had fifteen years' experience as Supervising Architect of the Treasury Department in Washington. William H. Lawrence was named as executive officer.

In 1912 there was another loss to the Department in the death of Despradelle, who had been in charge of design. His place was filled temporarily by Eugene J. A. Duquesne of Harvard. Some exchange between the two schools had already existed, for Despradelle in the later years of his teaching had given instruction at Harvard. Duquesne was assisted by Edgar I. Williams, a graduate of M.I.T. and a Fellow of the American Academy in Rome, who had also studied in Paris. Williams was succeeded briefly in 1916 by Stephen Codman '90, a former associate of Despradelle. Albert LeMonnier came to M.I.T. in 1913 from Paris and the Ecole des Beaux-Arts, but his stay was curtailed after one year by recall to France for military service. To take the place of Allen H. Cox, who had resigned, William T. Aldrich (Class of 1901 and student appointed instructors in design.

Ralph Adams Cram was appointed senior Professor of Architecture. He was at the time a member of the firm of Ferguson, Cram and Goodhue, and a noted author in his own right. Cram, who remained until 1922, brought to the Department his aggressive belief in Gothic architecture which had informed his own style of design.[49] Resignations continued with those of Ross Turner, instructor in water color since 1884; Truman H. Bartlett, instructor in modeling since 1891; and Samuel W. Mead, who had come to the Department in 1893 as assistant to Despradelle.

Steps had been taken to strengthen the structural studies by making changes in the Architectural Engineering option which placed it on the graduate level leading to a Master of Science in Architectural Engineering. Lawrence was in charge of this option which Chandler had favored and supported. In the four-year course, surveying was substituted for history of ornament. William F. Brown added a course in water color to his successful drawing classes, and Alexander S. Jenney was appointed to take charge of the courses in professional relations and in working drawings and specifications.

Chandler left a vigorous and expanding Department of Architecture. The graduate course had been established officially with the Institute's granting of a Master of Science degree in 1893, later changed (in 1921) to Master in Architecture. Gifts and prizes, bestowed generously, had enabled the Department to reward outstanding students and to encourage others to pursue further studies through European travel. The Architectural Society Scholarship Fund became available for the first year in 1911. Two medals, one gold and one silver, to be awarded to winners in design problems had been donated by the Société des Architectes Diplomés par le Gouvernement Français. These were awarded for seven years, from 1913 to 1920. Joint problems with Harvard and the Boston Architectural Club had been assigned experimentally but discontinued after a few years.

46   The Interpower Trolley Car
      Station, submitted by Ken-
      neth E. Carpenter in 1910 as
      a *projet* for the Paris Prize,
      is a remarkable application of
      old forms to new techniques.
      The plan includes a large as-
      sembly hall and several lec-
      ture rooms and banquet halls,
      all capped with an elaborate
      dome. It epitomizes the aca-
      demic thinking of an age that
      was in the process of out-
      stripping eclecticism but had
      not come to grips with new
      demands of transportation,
      industry, or communication.
      The use of electricity was
      making rapid strides—along
      with other technologies—
      while the profession of archi-
      tecture, except for a few
      isolated individuals, was com-
      placently living in a leisurely
      and genteel past.

The scheme of study at M.I.T. as formulated during Chandler's leadership was tailored to the demands of practicing architects. Many offices were directed by graduates of the Ecole des Beaux-Arts, who favored the Paris influence. Chandler's belief that design instructors should be actively engaged in the practice of architecture or have had previous professional experience helped to relate teaching to thinking of the time. The World's Fair in 1893 had ushered in another neoclassic trend with visions of the City Beautiful as a group of Parthenons, shining white and surmounted by gods and goddesses in flowing marble robes. History and literature were considered basic to the understanding use of precedent and formed a foundation for developing appreciation of architecture as a fine art. Professional work began in the first year with a course in freehand drawing that was continued throughout the program, progressing from exercises in details of casts to decorative figure design, considered appropriate at that time to beautify the exteriors of buildings. The Museum of Fine Arts in Boston permitted regular classes to be held in its galleries. Drawing was supplemented by courses in water color, pen, and pencil; composition and rendering; and modeling in clay. Design and history of architecture were begun in the second year so that the principles of classical proportion could become part of the student's vocabulary in composition. Lectures on the orders were accompanied by a course in shades and shadows.

History of architecture was followed by history of European civilization and art, a course that became more elaborate with the years as it attempted to survey in entirety the fields of painting and sculpture. Again, the resources of the Museum of Fine Arts were made available for class study, while the excellent collection of the Art Department in the Boston Public Library was put at the disposal of students in the course. Final instruction in historical styles was given in ornament, with the objective of developing facility in inventing colorful and decorative designs. Architectural history and European civilization and art were scheduled to run parallel with design and to one another, while Cram's course in philosophy of architecture

was intended to interlace the structure of the curriculum,
making architecture meaningful as the finest expression
of various cultures.

Construction was taught in several courses: applied
mechanics, graphical statistics, and strength of materials.
These were followed by constructive design, which was
intended to teach application of theory to practical problems that might arise in architectural practice. Perspective
and stereotomy were taught in the third year. A course in
building stones was considered important, and visits were
made to quarries in the vicinity of Boston. Heating and
ventilation were taught as practical subjects requiring a
thorough knowledge of existing methods. Instruction in
working drawings and specifications was carried to a point
where students would be familiar with office procedures
and able to learn through actual practice. In fact, work
in an architect's office during summer vacations was encouraged in order to complete the preparation for a career
in architecture.

In general, the course in architecture at M.I.T. con-
formed to the criteria established by the Committee on
Education of the American Institute of Architects: that education should be posed on a broad cultural base and should
maintain constant contact between theory and practice.
The American Institute of Architects also believed in a
practice that stemmed directly from the French school: that
judgment and criticisms of problems should be made by
professors not in charge of the particular assignment. To
this end, visiting lecturers and architects contributed their
practical opinions to class work. The American Institute of
Architects had also recommended stimulation of aptitude
through interscholastic competition, and M.I.T. had joined
with other colleges for a trial run. Competing in this venture were Harvard, the University of Pennsylvania, Columbia, and Cornell; but M.I.T. withdrew after two years when
the results proved to be less satisfactory than anticipated.

The Architectural Society of M.I.T., founded in 1886,
had been a lively organization, holding regular meetings,
inviting speakers active in the profession, and embarking
on various enterprises intended to benefit its members.

50

One of its major projects had been tracing plates from rare volumes that could be duplicated as blueprints and sold at cost. Each student devoted three hours a week to tracing, until the early years of the twentieth century brought more rapid means of reproduction by photography and magazines began to publish illustrations of ancient buildings.

Ambitiously, the Society had also printed an *Architectural Annual,*[50] a series of volumes of presentations submitted for the bachelor and master degrees. The *Annual* also reproduced freehand work, ornamental details, and examples of figure drawing. The series was discontinued for lack of adequate financial support after the 1904-05 volume, but in 1907 the Architectural Society launched a new venture, *The Technology Architectural Record.* Published quarterly, the *Record* enlarged on the *Annual* by including pertinent editorials, notes on alumni, and brief articles related to class study. Although the *Record* survived for only ten years, its calibre earned it the right to represent the Department officially, and copies were sent to prospective students.

Graduates of the Department's early years were carrying its precepts to other schools from New York to California. Alfred D. F. Hamlin, well-known architectural historian, received a degree from M.I.T. in 1878, went to Columbia University to teach in Ware's new school, and later succeeded Ware as head of the school. H. Langford Warren, a student at M.I.T. for two years, was invited to teach a course at Harvard University in 1893. When a school of architecture was later established, Warren became dean. He returned to M.I.T. briefly in 1916-17 to teach the history course. Frederick M. Mann '94 took part in the formation of no less than three schools: he organized a professional curriculum at Washington University in 1902, eight years later resigned to direct the already growing department at the University of Illinois, and finally went on to establish a school of architecture at the University of Minnesota, which he led until his resignation in 1936. Henry McGood-

The rendering of A Church Organ, by John T. Arms, Jr., 1911, was a problem in third-year design. Presented in pencil and water color, it portrays the excellence of craftsmanship that was to take Arms to the height of success as an etcher. Collections of his work are to be found in numerous museums in the United States, Canada, and London.

52 The drawings of An Opera House, by John T. Arms, 1911, on this and the following page, are examples of the fine draftsmanship that Despradelle could exact from his students; but these are also something more than splendid renderings—they are the beginning of a life-long devotion to etching. In beauty of line and delicacy of detail, Arms' Opera House shows early evidence of the qualities that were to inform his later work. Drawn in pencil with faint wash for shadows, the result is a richly ornamented façade embellished with almost every classic ornament.

Section of An Opera House,
by John Taylor Arms, 1911.

win '94, also teaching at Washington University, was called
to the Department of Architecture at Carnegie Institute
of Technology in 1907; in 1912 he succeeded Henry Horn-
bostel as head of the Department. Prescott A. Hopkins '92
took charge of the program in architecture at the Georgia
School of Technology for its first year, 1908-1909. Ellis F.
Lawrence '01 organized the School of Architecture and
Allied Arts at the University of Oregon in 1914, where he
remained as dean for many years. Emil Lorch '93 established a professional course in architecture at the University of Michigan in 1906 and later became dean when
a separate school was created. Frederick E. Giesecke '04
served for many years as head of the Department of
Architecture at the University of Texas, and Cecil F. Baker
'07 directed departments of architecture at both Kansas
State College and the University of Cincinnati. A. Lawrence
Kocher '13 was head of the Department of Architecture at
Pennsylvania State College for sixteen years before becoming an editor of *Architectural Record*. Robert R. Taylor '92
directed architectural instruction at Tuskegee Institute.

The Beaux-Arts influence was carried to the West Coast
by John Galen Howard, who had studied five years in
Paris after his graduation from M.I.T. in 1886. Howard, as
a result of placing third in the Phoebe A. Hearst competition for the development of the University of California,
had been requested to direct the planning of the campus.
Through necessity of training his own assistants he had
formed a small *atelier* in his office that, in 1904, became
the nucleus of a Department of Architecture of the University of California.

Later graduates who took leading roles in education
were Edmund S. Campbell '06[51] and Allen H. Kimball '11.
Kimball in 1914, took charge of the Department of Structural Design at Iowa State College, which was later changed
to the Department of Architectural Engineering. Campbell,
who had also received his master's degree from M.I.T.,
went immediately to the Carnegie Institute of Technology
and then became head of the rapidly developing Department of Architecture at Armour Institute of Technology.
This department had adopted an undergraduate curriculum

55

with technical courses at Armour Institute and fine arts courses at the Art Institute in Chicago. From Armour, Campbell went to New York City in 1924 as Dean of the Beaux-Arts Institute of Design, and in 1927 he became head of the School of Art and Architecture at the University of Virginia where he remained until his death in 1950.

After Taylor's resignation, William H. Lawrence became chairman of the Department from 1914 to 1919. Ralph Adams Cram, who came to M.I.T. in 1914, succeeded Lawrence, interrupting the Beaux-Arts dynasty until 1922, when he left and William Emerson became director of the Department. A course in applied perspective, which was intended to aid students in three-dimensional visualization, replaced clay modeling. Pen and pencil rendering disappeared from the curriculum with the resignation of David A. Gregg after twenty-six years of teaching. Cram directed instruction in design and found the Institute a testing ground—as well as a battle-ground—for the theories propounded during his years as chairman of the Committee on Education of the American Institute of Architects. Lectures by practicing architects and men well qualified to speak on other professions gave practical reality to the course in professional relations. Langford Warren of the Harvard School of Architecture, with Ida Loring as assistant, was appointed to teach the course in architectural history. Warren lived to teach for only one year and was succeeded by Eliot T. Putnam, also of Harvard and a student of the Ecole des Beaux-Arts. Ida Loring became Librarian, remaining until 1929, and she continued to assist in the history course as an authority on Gothic.

Recognition of the rank of the Department came from both the Corporation of M.I.T. and from outside sources in the years just before World War I. The Corporation, in response to repeated requests, made available a $1,000 Traveling Fellowship as an annual award, thus supporting Chandler's belief in the benefits of a year of travel. The Boston Society of Architects established the William E. Chamberlain Prize, in memory of Chamberlain of the Class

The Pantheon by Louis C. Rosenberg (see also the frontispiece) is a typical class exercise of the year 1913. But Rosenberg flamboyantly decorated the classic form and brought the whole presentation to life by sending two processions marching up the stairs with banners flying. Although Rosenberg continued to pursue a career in architecture, he has become noted as an etcher and illustrator of books, with many of his works represented in museums, libraries, and colleges.

"The proper use of precedent" for professional training in architecture was meticulously applied by Louis C. Rosenberg in his Estate on an Island, 1913. While a faithful reproduction of a villa replete with pavilions, gardens, terraces, fountains, cypresses, and hedges, the drawing has a force and originality foreshadowing the talent of his later work.

of 1877, for fifth-year students. And finally, a substantial gift of money was received from Mrs. Harriet A. Henshaw of London in memory of her brother, Frank Walter Boles, the income of which was available for the purchase of books, slides, and other materials in the field of fine arts.

Attendance had not yet been decimated by the threat of war; in the academic year of 1913-14 enrollment reached 160 students, the largest in the history of the Department. The increase brought the inevitable problems of overcrowded drafting rooms—but this time there was a solution.

The Institute had now completed the new buildings in Cambridge, designed by Welles W. Bosworth of the Class of 1889, a successful architect who had enhanced his training with years of study in Europe. In calling upon one of its own graduates, M.I.T. expressed its confidence in its alumni—a confidence that is by no means common to all colleges and universities that train architects. The Bosworth plan—to combine neoclassical appearance with a flexible arrangement of individual yet connected buildings centered on courts—was an ingenious scheme to permit circulation through interior corridors and to allow for future expansion of interlocking units. The central rotunda dominated a great court reminiscent of Jefferson's plan for the University of Virginia.

The major part of the Institute moved into its new quarters in Cambridge, and the Rogers Building on Boylston Street in Boston, where the Department of Architecture held its first classes in 1868, was once again available. With its handsome French Renaissance facade and its spacious and dignified interior, the Rogers Building was admirably adapted to the purpose and ideals of the Department.

However, World War I soon reduced the Department to about one-third of its usual complement. The staff took the opportunity to schedule conferences with Harvard and the Boston Architectural Club to explore educational methods and to give practitioners and teachers an opportunity to discuss the critical area of academic training in relation to office practice. Collaborative problems were tried again for a number of years with Harvard and the

Isle of Spice

An Isle of Spice, by Frank S. Whearty, 1914, was a plan for an amusement center on an island. Inspired by the Midway Gardens in Chicago designed by Frank Lloyd Wright the previous year, the center was of the same tawny color and similar layout. Pleasure gardens had played but a small part in the social life of the United States, although they were not unknown in New York and Philadelphia. The World's Fair of 1893, with its air of gaiety and out-door amusements, had brought a sense of freedom and enchantment to the people, but when they returned to their homes they preferred to sit on their front porches or stroll through the parks that were being laid out in almost all the major cities.

Boston Architectural Club but were abandoned when Harvard withdrew from the venture. M.I.T. then joined with several other colleges in interscholastic problems that were considered a means of broadening the students' approach to design.

After the war, in the summer of 1922, seven architecture students joined the American Students' Reconstruction Unit[52] to aid French architects and engineers in replanning and rebuilding the devastated regions of France. The Unit consisted of 50 students from fifteen colleges, including also four engineers from M.I.T. Expenses were met by funds raised by alumni. The Unit, which placed its services at the disposal of the Ministry of the Liberated Regions, made topographical surveys, prepared measured drawings of ruined structures, and prepared plans for new buildings.

George B. Ford, a graduate of the Class of 1900, was chosen by the French government as consultant in rebuilding cities and towns destroyed in the war. Ford had graduated from Harvard before coming to M.I.T. and later studied at the Ecole des Beaux-Arts. His architectural experience as member of George B. Post and Sons and his interest in the esthetic and social values of city planning led to his leadership in city planning. He was elected president of the American City Planning Institute, served as adviser to numerous American communities, and was selected general director of the Regional Plan Association, Inc., of New York.

The restrained classicism of An Entrance Portico for a Pantheon, by Ernest A. Grunsfeld, Jr., 1915-16, indicates the fine quality that could be achieved when the proportions of a building were in correct relationship and when the decorative elements were scaled to each part of the whole. The bronze doors, which appear to have the same patterns as the originals, and replicas of other classic systems are all harmoniously integrated. The lines indicating the total structure convey the impression of the vast monumentality of Hadrian's round temple in Rome.

About fifteen schools of architecture were founded in the decade following World War I. Walter T. Rolfe '23 shared in the formative years of two schools. At North Dakota State College he was head of the Department of Architecture from 1924 to 1928. He then left for the University of Texas, where he taught for twenty-two years, serving from 1935 until 1946 as chairman of the Department of Architecture. Another M.I.T. graduate, Homer B. Huntoon '28, succeeded Rolfe at North Dakota. Three other schools were directed by M.I.T. graduates of the Thirties. Elliot L. Whitaker '31 was director of the School of Architecture and Landscape Architecture at Ohio State University from 1950 to 1955. Thomas K. Fitzpatrick '33 taught in several colleges, including M.I.T., before going to Charlottesville in 1953 to become Dean of the School of Architecture at the University of Virginia. Harlan E. McClure '41, who studied in Europe and traveled extensively before establishing his own practice in Minneapolis, became head of the Department of Architecture at Clemson College in 1955 and dean when the School of Architecture was created there in 1958.

In Canada, the School of Architecture at the University of Manitoba has for a number of years been under the direction of John A. Russell, who received his bachelor's and master's degrees in architecture from M.I.T. in 1928 and 1932, respectively.

Architectural training has also proved its value in other fields of art through several young men who left M.I.T. during the war years and later became pre-eminent in their chosen professions. Samuel V. Chamberlain '18 is now best known throughout the country as author and photographer, although he is also noted as etcher and lithographer. John Taylor Arms '11 and Louis C. Rosenberg '13 also became noted etchers as did George C. Wales, who graduated in 1889. Arthur L. Guptill '16, writer of popular textbooks on art, was co-founder and president of the Watson-Guptill Publications, Inc.

In addition to individual achievements, alumni of the Department maintained a persistent loyalty and energy in organizing, in 1916, a Society of Technology Architects. The Constitution[53] states its objective as furthering "the well-being of the Department of Architecture by fostering the interest of the members in the Department and each other." The Society published an informative *Bulletin* through 1924. Subsequent issues appeared quarterly as inserts in *The Technology Review* from February, 1925, to July, 1926.

The close of World War I found the Department of Architecture with a new leader, William Emerson, who remained until the beginning of the next war. His span of office, 1919 to 1939, covered a period that brought both opportunities and problems, as he himself wrote many years later. Emerson was a logical successor to the office once occupied by William Robert Ware, as he had studied for two years at Columbia University during Ware's administration after graduating from Harvard. He then went to Paris for three years of study at the Ecole des Beaux-Arts. Returning to New York City, Emerson opened an office and built numerous private houses and tenements. To the latter he gave much thought and study in order to improve the living conditions of low-salaried workers. An active member of the American Institute of Architects, Emerson brought to his position two years' experience as chairman of the Committee on Education.

Several concepts were stressed repeatedly in the annual reports that appeared over Emerson's signature. Together with other members of the staff, Emerson constantly urged lengthening the period of study required for the bachelor's degree from four to five years, as was being done at other colleges. Permission for this change was granted in 1931.

New subjects were then added to the curriculum: theory of color, architectural administration, architectural humanities, and town planning; others, architectural history and theory of architecture, were transferred to the first year in order to present to the student the essentials of his profession at the very beginning of his career. Architectural humanities, town planning, and landscape architecture formed a group of studies primarily for graduate students. The purpose of the five-year program was to allow time

Samuel V. Chamberlain studied at M.I.T. before going to London and Paris to continue his training in art; he has now become famous throughout America for photographs, etchings, and lithographs perpetuating a charming and romantic image of villages and landscapes. The fine quality of Chamberlain's early work appears in the renderings reproduced on this and the following pages which he made for the Sub-Committee on the Form of Memorial to Soldiers, Sailors, and Marines, to be Erected by the City of Boston. The Memorial was devised by a group of Boston architects who, in 1921, prepared an elaborate plan for an island in the Charles River as a site for a symmetrical building group composed of carillon tower, open-air theater, and two flanking wings. The remainder of the island was to be developed as a water park.

for more thorough study of essential subjects. But the advantage of the extra year was not apparent until the program had gone into effect and the quality of thesis work was found to have improved.

A summer course in office practice was made a requirement for a degree in architecture in order to circumvent the perennial problem of making good draftsmen, familiar with office practice, at the expense of other studies. William Lawrence took charge of the former Department of Drawing which became the Division of Drawing within the Department of Architecture, a reorganization for the purpose of adapting drawing directly to the needs of students in architecture.

"That a carefully considered policy in the teaching of design was essential to the future success of the Department was obvious," Emerson wrote in his first report as head of the Department, "and a matter of agreement between the staff and President Maclaurin."[54] In a later paper Emerson stated that "an essential feature in the teaching of design is the coordination of this all-important subject with related courses."[55] To this end, teachers in other subjects, notably construction, shared in the criticism of design problems, and criticisms were scheduled on a regular basis of two each week. Outside lecturers were regarded as stimulating to the Department, and for the same reason students were encouraged to participate in the competitions of the Society of Beaux-Arts Architects in New York City, where they won high places for a number of years.

To head the teaching of design Emerson chose Albert Ferran, a graduate of the Ecole des Beaux-Arts and winner of the *Grand Prix de Rome,* but he returned to France after only one year. His successor was Jacques Carlu, who remained at M.I.T. from 1924 until 1933. Carlu,[56] also a Grand Prix scholar, had won a number of competitions in Europe. In 1910 he went to Rumania, where he successfully competed in the design for the Palais du Sénat in Bucharest. In this country Carlu came to be recognized as a distinguished draftsman and painter with several murals to his credit. As director of Architecture at the Fontainebleau School of Fine Arts during the summer months, Carlu inevitably

Longitudinal Section

Scale

Principal Facade

When it became fashionable to build a country estate, the popular architect needed a varied vocabulary of styles to satisfy the whim of his client. Lester I. Beal's Aviary, 1918, for the second-year design course would well have suited the popular demand for dwellings, conservatories, and teahouses faithfully copied from those in Europe or the Orient. It was the era of the fantastic Florida villa and the transplanted castle with rooms replete with woodwork and furnishings from Europe.

72

A Central School of Fine Arts, by Franklin A. Bermingham, 1918, is a beautiful example of the Beaux-Arts influence that dominated both architectural education and a large segment of the architectural profession for the next ten years.

influenced several students at M.I.T. to study at Fontainebleau during their vacations. M.I.T. students won the Paris Prize (Lloyd Warren Scholarship) three times during Carlu's term of teaching; in all, the Prize has been awarded to five M.I.T. students—Frederic C. Hirons '03, Donald S. Nelson '26, Joseph D. Murphy '29, Lawrence B. Anderson '30, and Maurice W. Kleinmann '33. Ernest N. Gelotte '23, who had practical experience on building projects in the Boston area, began teaching a course in construction in 1930 that has become structural analysis in the present curriculum. John Lyon Reid '31 joined the staff in the following year and remained until 1946.

Throughout his administration William Emerson sought

74

A

COMMERCIAL

BUILDING

·ELEVATION·
·SCALE ⅛"=1'-0"·

·PERSPECTIVE·
·SCALE ⅛"=1'-0"·

12

This building by Ellsworth V. Holden, 1920, could well have been included in the 281 entries placed before the final jury for the Chicago Tribune Tower competition of 1922, and it could well have been awarded the winning prize. Such was the taste of the jury for vertical lines soaring to a parapet and ornate tower. Holden's formula was the formula of the New York skyscrapers, not of the Sullivan, Jenney, or Root concepts that had already appeared in Chicago.

every means of providing opportunities for travel for his students. Through his friends and acquaintances, Emerson established channels of communication in France, England, and Italy so that students and alumni would find a cordial and helpful reception in such places as the *atelier* of Georges Gromort in Paris, the Architectural Association in London, and the American Academy in Rome. Emerson persuaded M.I.T. to become a contributing member of the American School of Classical Studies in Athens, as he believed in the value of archeological research for students in architecture. In fact, Emerson's interest in antiquity led to research and the publication of several scholarly papers.

In an annual report written toward the end of Emerson's term as dean, President Compton reviewed the program of the School in relation to the profession of architecture and future requirements of its practitioners.[57] Design was to remain the "central theme of all good architecture," but it was acknowledged that "the techniques of its application must continually adapt themselves to the evolution of the technical and social environment." The School had made the last of its four moves into a new building adjoining the Cambridge group in 1938, and President Compton recommended that in its new location closer to the technological and scientific schools of M.I.T., the School "capitalize and coördinate as effectively as possible our existing strong programs in design and in the various technical aspects of construction and equipment of buildings."

Emerson took initial steps to adjust design courses to conditions encountered in actual practice by means of specialized seminars and projects. The Department of Building Engineering and Construction cooperated in the technical aspects of constructing a Faculty Club. Other problems involved lighting, building materials, and other elements basic to a new theory of architectural design. Emerson sought also to provide opportunities for office experience for undergraduates during the summer months. The conservative ideal of design as the dominant subject in architectural education that had ruled M.I.T., as well as other American schools, was beginning to yield to contemporary trends in actual practice.

This design by John F. G.
Gunther, 1923, is typical of
the eclectic age that was
about to disappear.

During Emerson's term of office the field of city planning
was introduced, first by lectures and design problems and
later by an organized curriculum leading to both the
bachelor's and master's degrees.[58] Sir Raymond Unwin and
Thomas Adams, pioneers and eminent planners from
England, took part in organizing a course of study and
donated much valuable material. Thomas Adams had come
to New York to direct the monumental Regional Plan of
New York and Its Environs. A reorganization of the Department of Architecture was effected in 1932 that changed it
to a School, with William Emerson as dean. City planning
became a division within the School; Frederick J. Adams,
son of Thomas Adams, was appointed as its head, and that
fall the division first offered a five-year course leading to
the degree of Bachelor of Architecture in city planning. This
was the second college program in city planning; the first
had been introduced at Harvard University in 1925.

The following statements, from a description of courses
in city planning published in 1935,[59] described the philosophy of the program:

*The purpose of the courses in city planning at the Institute
is to provide a basic training in the fundamental principles
and technique of city planning and civic design. The curriculum is based on a recognition of the fact that the solutions of all planning problems—whether of city, region, or
state—depend on the proper co-ordination of all the factors
involved—not only those in the fields of architecture and
engineering but also the economic, sociological, and governmental factors.*

Frederick J. Adams, who came to M.I.T. to direct the
city planning division, was born in London, attended the
Royal Naval College of Canada for three years, studied for
one year at McGill University and four years at the Architectural Association in London, and received his bachelor's
degree in architecture from Columbia University in 1928.
He came to M.I.T. after several years' experience in the
offices of architects and city planners in New York City.

Government attention to planning at various administrative levels during the Thirties created a demand for men qualified to determine broad policies and capable of making decisions with far-reaching effects. The Division of City Planning,[60] therefore, geared itself to producing graduates of a high calibre through constant revitalization of its courses. In 1935 a graduate program leading to the degree of Master in City Planning was added. Experts in the profession were invited to lecture and to criticize problems and designs. The cooperation of several local and regional agencies in New England enabled students to acquire experience in the field for the course in city planning practice. A summer planning conference was inaugurated in conjunction with the Harvard Graduate School of Design, and M.I.T. later conducted its own program, which still attracts capacity enrollment. The first Traveling Fellowship for a year's study of planning in the United States and Europe was awarded in 1936 to John Tasker Howard, who later became head of the Department.

In 1938, one year before his retirement, Emerson also saw the completion of a project that he had been urging for ten years. An appropriation was made for first- and second-year students, supervised by faculty members, to buy a plot of land and design a small family house. Every step—surveying the land, preparation of working drawings and specifications, and erection of the house—was student-directed for the purpose of gaining practical experience.

Emerson retired in 1939 after directing the School through twenty years of changes and innovations. The Architectural Engineering option had been discontinued in the preceding year with the retirement of William H. Lawrence. Courses had been revised and added. Concepts new to traditional thinking were being explored, such as abstract design and industrial design. Seminars in acoustics, illumination, construction, and materials were inaugurated for graduate students. The construction of models had been adopted in all grades to develop a three-dimensional approach to problems in design. Lawrence B. Anderson '30, who joined the M.I.T. faculty in 1933, exchanged positions

Regional expression in architecture was slow to take root in America and slower to appear in architectural schools. But J. Fred Buenz, a student from Texas, adopted for A Summer School of Fine Arts, 1926, a Spanish style that was being recalled about that time in the Southwest.

with Professor Roy Childs Jones of the University of Minnesota, the beginning of an exchange program that expanded in later years from a domestic to an international basis. The library, in new quarters arranged on the alcove plan on an entire floor of the School's new building, had been enriched by gifts of books and slides and was becoming a good reference collection. Ida Loring, assistant in architectural history, served as librarian for twenty-six years, succeeded from 1929 to 1948 by Florence W. Stiles '22. In 1948 Margaret H. Beale was named librarian *pro tem* to work closely with the faculty of city planning in building a collection in that field of literature, and in 1951 she was succeeded by Caroline Shillaber. Gifts had made foreign travel possible for two more students, and a large donation, given anonymously, aided students who showed unusual promise for their chosen career.

An M.I.T. graduate of 1903, Walter R. MacCornack, succeeded William Emerson in 1939, but remained as dean for only five years. MacCornack, an architect from Cleveland, Ohio, had specialized in schools and large-scale housing projects. He had learned to know M.I.T. as a member of the Advisory Committee for the School of Architecture for eight years preceding his appointment.

MacCornack accepted the proposals of the teaching staff to revise the curriculum in order to strengthen courses in principles of construction, building materials and their uses, practical economics of the building industry, and the fundamental principles of city planning. He permitted the first hint of the modern trend or functional architecture, as it was then called, to appear in the classrooms, when in 1940-41 he brought Alvar Aalto of Finland to M.I.T. as Research Professor in Architecture. Until that time, Aalto's fresh, clear, rhythmic architecture had appeared only in the minor Finnish Pavilion for the New York World's Fair and in the exhibition of his work at the Museum of Modern Art. Aalto returned to M.I.T. in 1948 to teach and to design an imaginative new dormitory of dark red brick and undulating walls, now known as the Everett Moore Baker House.

Aid and incentive to research programs came to the School from the heirs of Albert Farwell Bemis '93, who

A Restaurant in the Air, by Joseph D. Murphy, won a Second Medal in the competition of the Beaux-Arts Institute of Design in 1929. The problem was to design a restaurant in the air in a park that would have views of the surrounding landscape. Although the year was 1929, the Institute cautioned students to remember "that the unusual developments of steel and reinforced concrete make possible this type of structure."

82 A Concert Hall, by Frederic
A. Pawley, 1930, expressed a
freedom and movement away
from classicism that was appearing in the Thirties. The
auditorium was undecorated
except for colored lights that
could be projected to play
over the ceilings and walls
creating abstract, fantastic, or
even architectural forms.

A CONCERT HALL

established in 1938 the Foundation which bears his name.
Bemis (1879-1936), who was founder and head of Bemis industries, was long active in the affairs of the Institute and was a member of its Corporation from 1914 until his death in 1936. He had a deep and personal interest in the problems of shelter. In collaboration with John E. Burchard '23, he wrote the three-volume study *The Evolving House* (1933-36), a scholarly work which reviewed the history and evolution of the house and investigated the housing industry as a field for mass production. The Foundation established in his name was dedicated to the "search for, and dissemination of, knowledge pertaining to adequate, economical, and more abundant shelter."

The Bemis Foundation made possible an active program in research for many years and produced numerous publications. Burchard was its first director, serving from 1938 to 1948; he then became director of Libraries and later dean of the School of Humanities and Social Science. His successor as Foundation director was Burnham Kelly,[61] who also taught the legal aspects of city planning. Professor Kelly received his master's degree in city planning from M.I.T. in 1941, following earlier study at Williams College and Harvard Law School. As director of the Foundation until 1954, he conducted several successful conferences on housing and wrote the now classic book, *The Prefabrication of Houses,* published in 1950. The Foundation investigated, by experiment and study, methods of construction and prefabrication, acquiring in the process an historical archive of printed and manuscript material. With the termination of its research activities in 1954, its funds became available for lecturers from the United States and overseas, a plan which has brought many noted architects, writers, and designers to the School for one or more semesters.

84

A Farm Group by Wilfred J.
Pucke, 1942, was an adaptation of the then-popular Med-
iterranean style of rural
building.

BUTTER & MILK

CHEESE

1st Mention Placed

A FARM GROUP

W. J. PUCKE
A FARM GROUP. NOV 4 '32
M. I. T.

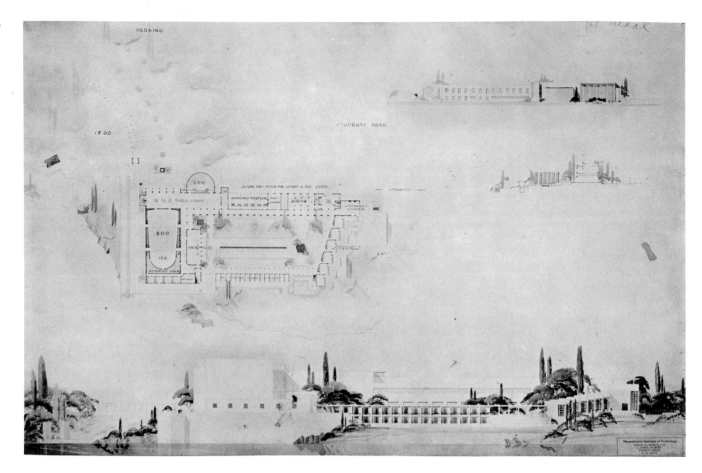

A School of Music by Nemb-
hard N. Culin, 1934, speaks
for itself in expressing a
changed and changing attitude toward design. The arrangement of interlocking
volumes, the layout of public
and private areas around a
court for easy circulation, and
the provision for a park and
parking area characterized an
attempt to solve each problem in fresh terms. Consideration of spaces and volumes
and their interrelationships
were part of the evolving
trend in architecture.

In the Twenties and Thirties, schools of architecture, like the profession, were beginning to feel the effects of architectural styles emerging in this country as a result of new technologies. Impatience with classic training was permeating the schools,[62] while at the same time there was hesitation in following new leaders. Harvard had invited Walter Gropius in 1938 to teach its advanced course in design. Germany, which had been the first country of the Industrial Revolution to train young minds in the application of science to industry, was again one of the leaders in new methods of education to adapt new concepts and new materials in building. The Bauhaus, established by Gropius in Germany, was oriented to teaching architecture as a unity of arts and crafts expressed through the media of new industrial techniques. Other members of the Bauhaus group also brought its influence to America, notably Laszlo Moholy-Nagy, who founded the Institute of Design in Chicago. But the Bauhaus influence never dominated the architectural thinking of the time, as there were strong indigenous forces at work within the country in the philosophies of Frank Lloyd Wright, Eliel Saarinen, and Richard Neutra.

The international competition held in 1922 for the Chicago Tribune Tower had evoked more significant designs than were, at the time, realized. A project submitted by Walter Gropius and Adolf Meyer seemed striking to America in its stripped simplicity, yet such buildings were not uncommon in Europe. Eliel Saarinen's design received high commendation for its slender elegance, but it was a Gothic tower by John M. Howells and Raymond M. Hood that won the competition. Both architects were M.I.T. graduates (1890 and 1903, respectively), and both had received diplomas from the Ecole des Beaux-Arts.

The Ecole was then the dominating influence on American architectural education. In addition to Ecole-trained Americans, there was an influx of Frenchmen into the schools. Harvard had Duquesne and Jean-Jacques Haffner, Paul Phillippe Cret and Jacques Gréber taught at the University of Pennsylvania, Jean Hebrard and others at

Cornell, Maurice J. Prevot at Columbia, Gabriel Ferrand and C. E. Grapin at Carnegie Institute of Technology, and Jean Labatut at Princeton; and as many more came to other schools in the United States. All were excellent designers in the classical manner. But they gave no consideration to building for the country's emerging needs: new types of factories, larger office buildings, mass housing, and more schools. Individual dwelling houses were for the most part still on the opulent scale and in the eclectic style of those of the Nineties. Exceptions to the long-imitative styles were visible, however, in various regions of the country and were especially conspicuous in California, where climate and landscape were being recognized as factors in the design of a house. One of the architects exploring an independent style was William Wilson Wurster, chosen by M.I.T. in 1944 as dean of its School of Architecture and Planning. Then studying city planning at Harvard, Dean Wurster had already earned a place as one of the forward-looking architects of the West. As dean, he brought a breath of fresh air to the curriculum. By means of visiting lecturers he infused the School with new life and new interest. He made numerous appointments to the faculty of men who directed its policies into completely new and progressive channels.

Administrative changes effected during Dean Wurster's administration were beneficial in developing and improving professional curricula in both architecture and planning. A School of Architecture and Planning was established in 1944 with two coordinate departments: Architecture, under the direction of Lawrence B. Anderson; and City and Regional Planning, under the direction of Frederick J. Adams.

As a teacher and administrator, Professor Anderson has guided effectively and tactfully the policies of a program that has emerged from Beaux-Arts domination to a forceful and foremost role in architectural education. He has taken a leading part in the affairs of the Association of Collegiate Schools of Architecture and has worked unceasingly to improve the quality of both teachers and students. In partnership with Herbert L. Beckwith, who received a Master in Architecture from M.I.T. in 1926 and joined the faculty in the same year, he founded Anderson, Beckwith and Haible, a firm that has built several buildings on the M.I.T. campus and has been responsible for countless projects from New England to Manila. Professor Anderson (B.S. in Arch. 1927, University of Minnesota) taught for two years at the University of Virginia and then came to M.I.T. as a graduate student to earn his master's degree in architecture after one year, 1929-30. He won the Paris Prize in the year of his graduation and studied in Paris at the Ecole des Beaux-Arts for three years.

Dean Wurster chose Gyorgy Kepes to head the visual design courses. Professor Kepes had previously been in charge of drawing and color and of the Light Workshop at the Institute of Design in Chicago. In 1944 he published *Language of Vision,* a review of the art and the approach to art as taught at the Chicago Institute. Later, in 1956, Professor Kepes published *The New Landscape in Art and Science,*[63] a book of visual images and comments by various authors indicating a new aspect of perception based on scientific information and poetic vision. Born in Hungary and educated at the Royal Academy of Fine Arts, Professor Kepes had been head of the Light and Color Department at the New Bauhaus in Dessau before coming to this country, and was already known through many successful exhibitions of his paintings before he joined M.I.T. To Professor Kepes, the language of vision, by which he means optical communication, is the strongest means of orienting man in the new dimensions of his environment, of re-forming man into an integrated being. Professor Kepes has developed his courses in light and color as studies valuable to thinking in the three-dimensional world of the architect. A photographic workshop under his direction also enriches the training of architectural students, enabling them to observe more closely the world about themselves and to relate their ideas of structures to the human beings who will inhabit them.

Another addition to the faculty was Richard Filipowski, a native of Poland and former teacher at the Institute of Design in Chicago and the Harvard Graduate School of Design. In order to develop an esthetic vocabulary, Pro-

90

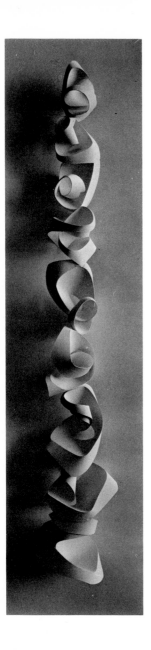

fessor Filipowski conducts studio courses in visual design to orient students' thinking of colors, textures, and materials in relation to buildings. In these courses students work with materials such as wood, plaster, metals, and plastics to generate an imaginative attitude toward the ordering of form and space.

Henry-Russell Hitchcock, the first architectural historian to recognize the "International Style," as he named it, was asked to teach the history course, which benefited not only from his encyclopaedic knowledge of past styles but also from his understanding interpretation of contemporary design in building. Hitchcock remained from 1946 until 1949.

In the fall of 1946 two more architects were added to the staff, Ralph Rapson and Carl Koch. Rapson had been trained at Cranbrook Academy[64] and had served as head of the Architecture Department at the Institute of Design in Chicago.[65] Koch, a Harvard School of Design graduate, had worked with such architects as Markelius, Stone, Gropius, and Breuer.

During Dean Wurster's tenure the Department of Architecture became involved in several very practical projects, including the design of temporary student housing for married veterans enrolled at M.I.T., a project directed by Robert Woods Kennedy who had joined the teaching staff in 1945. Another undertaking, sponsored by Godfrey L. Cabot funds, was a continuing research experiment to utilize solar energy in heating houses. Research houses were constructed and their performance tested while occupied by a small family. During the course of the experiments four houses have been built, the last one in Lexington in 1958.[66] The results of these experiments, carried on in conjunction with the Department of Civil Engineering, indicated that sunshine on the roof of a house in New England could be expected to supply two-thirds of the energy required for heating but that the cost of mechanical equipment required for such solar heating was higher than could be justified by fuel savings. A symposium on Space Heating with Solar Energy was held in 1950 and focused on direct utilization of solar energy as heat. Proceedings were subsequently published.

92   The outbreak of war in China in 1937 caused a tremendous migration of population. To effect a measure of control over innumerable temporary villages and towns, the Chinese government adopted a propaganda program to promote education, sanitation, social and economic reorganization, and a nationalistic spirit. Ieoh M. Pei's Bachelor's thesis, Standardized Propaganda Units for War Time and Peace Time China, 1940, was a plan for a unit revolving around a theater to capitalize on the Chinese people's extravagant fondness for theatrical presentations. The thesis, developed in cooperation with the Department of Civil Engineering, was unusual in the use of bamboo both architecturally and structurally.

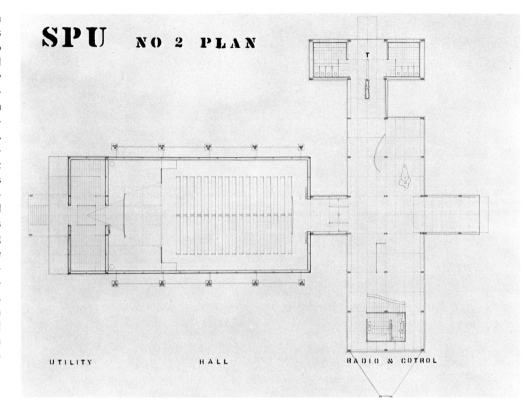

SPU NO 2 PLAN

UTILITY   HALL   RADIO & COTROL

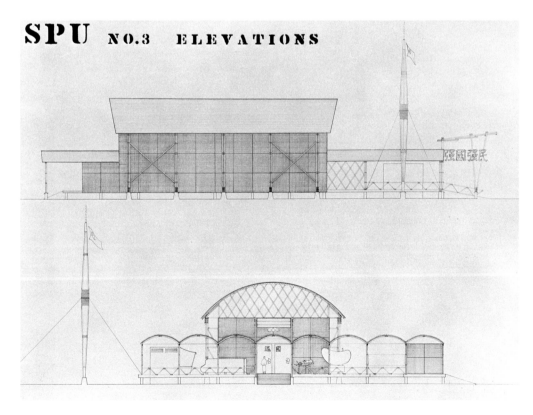

SPU NO.3 ELEVATIONS

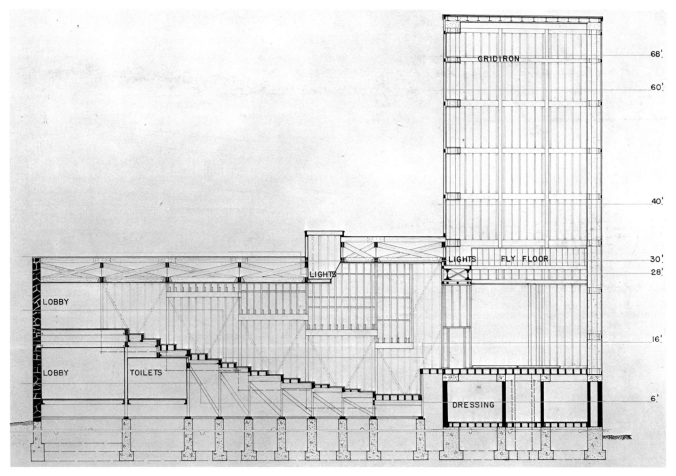

GRIDIRON

68'

60'

40'

LIGHTS   FLY FLOOR

30'

28'

LIGHTS

LOBBY

16'

LOBBY   TOILETS

DRESSING

6'

In A Theatre for Black Mountain College, 1943, Anatole Kopp undertook to provide a structure that could serve the community as well as the college. Although the College had a drama department it lacked a theater, and the town of Black Mountain, North Carolina, lacked a suitable building for concerts and lectures. With all these requirements in mind, Kopp in his Master's thesis planned a theater that would serve primarily for the study of theatrical arts and techniques as performed on a small stage.

When M.I.T. decided to sponsor, with a Boston insurance company, an apartment house for members of its staff and their families, it called upon the Department of Architecture to design a building. The result was Eastgate at 100 Memorial Drive, a collaborative effort on the part of Vernon A. DeMars (visiting critic), Ralph Rapson, William H. Brown, Carl Koch, and Robert W. Kennedy. The architects planned a building which faced the Charles River, with a balcony overlooking the river for every tenant. The arrangement of skip-flight elevators, a new device at the time, was adopted in order to reduce the cost of utilities and also to provide two-story apartments extending through the depth of the building.

Professional training in city and regional planning was established in eight other colleges and universities, in addition to Harvard and M.I.T., between 1932 and 1946. Although total enrollment was rising annually, the number of graduates was still below the national demand. At M.I.T. the Department of City and Regional Planning was expanding yearly under the direction of Professor Adams. Homer Hoyt and Lloyd Rodwin, experts in land economics, came to M.I.T. in 1944 and 1946 respectively; Hoyt remained only three years. Professor Rodwin has become an international authority on his subject, serving as consultant on housing and planning problems to many public and private organizations in this country and abroad. Roland B. Greeley, with experience in the National Resources Planning Board, joined the faculty in 1945; he resigned from teaching to assume an administrative post at the Institute in 1961. Flavel Shurtleff taught legal factors involved in planning from 1938 until he retired in 1951, returning annually, however, to participate in summer sessions. Charles Abrams, legal counsel in public and private housing law, brought to the Department the benefit of years of experience as lawyer, author, and lecturer. He was appointed in 1950 and has remained as Visiting Professor in Land Economics. Kevin Lynch, a graduate of the Department of Planning in 1947, joined the faculty in the following year; he had also studied at Frank Lloyd Wright's Taliesin. Professor Lynch was assigned at first to develop collaborative studies for the two departments of the School in order to foster the ability to work in teams to understand and solve the problems of both disciplines. Interweaving of courses in architecture and planning was considered desirable to promote a comprehensive attitude toward both subjects, but in subsequent years the tendency has been toward separating courses in the two fields.

There were important new educational demands in city and regional planning. Guiding urban and metropolitan growth now required men skilled in social, economic, and physical planning, and a background in legal and administrative aspects was becoming essential to interrelate policy making, analysis, and implementation in the total planning process.

A new four-year undergraduate course of study, with planning subjects beginning in the second year, replaced the five-year course in 1942 but was later discontinued.

Professor Adams was widely recognized for the steady progress and improvement of his Department and for his major role in the planning profession. He took part in activities of the League of Nations at Geneva and of the United Nations in New Delhi. His wisdom and perception as an educator were acknowledged in a commission by the Alfred Bettman Foundation to make a searching study of planning education in the United States. The penetrating analysis written by Professor Adams, *Urban Planning Education in the United States,* was published in 1954 by the Foundation in Cincinnati, Ohio. In addition to descriptive information on college-level planning courses throughout the country, there are chapters on the objectives and scope of urban planning, on the role of the planner, and on his training. Professor Adams wrote:

To meet present day requirements, the planner must be grounded in the social, economic, and physical aspects of urban development which must be integrated if an effective job of planning is to be done. The range of the required disciplines includes functional design, techniques of re-

*search, survey methods, economic analysis, public admin-
istration, and many more. While a highly developed skill
in one or more of these disciplines frequently proves valuable, a basic understanding of all aspects of the planning
process and their relationship to one another is even
more important if the planner is to play his full part in the
development of comprehensive plans for cities and regions.*

Since the inception of the planning course at M.I.T.,
the demand for graduates had annually exceeded the supply; graduates were being assigned increased responsibilities in staffing municipal, regional, and federal agencies,
and they were in demand as private consultants. The
techniques of planning were being recognized as valuable
to private business and industry as well as to governments
of metropolitan regions that were absorbing annually
hundreds of square miles of rural land.

These growing responsibilities of graduates required
constant reappraisal of courses and objectives in city and
regional planning education. Teaching and research were
demanding more personnel with more advanced training
than the nation's schools were graduating. The matter was
of grave concern to the profession as well as to the faculties
of schools, and the Department at M.I.T. undertook a critical restudy of its educational objectives.

One result was to discontinue the undergraduate program, which took place in 1954. The course of study was
then wholly on the graduate level, leading to the degree of
Master in City Planning. Additional resources for study
were made available through a cooperative arrangement
with Harvard University for cross-registration in courses.
Two years are usually required for completion of this program. Time is normally divided between workshop problems in city and regional planning, including a thesis, and
seminars and classes in such subjects as planning techniques, legislation, administration, housing, land economics, urban design, and theory and research.

A second step was to extend opportunities for advanced
study and research. In *A summary of the program and
objectives* . . . (1955), the Department noted at M.I.T. a

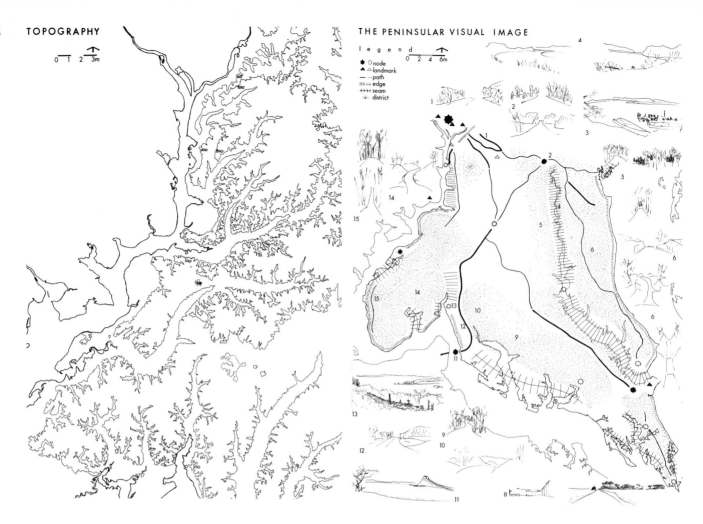

The plans on this and following pages represent a scheme for the development of the future form of southeast metropolitan Washington. Both staff and students in the Department of City and Regional Planning shared in the exploration of dealing with an underdeveloped segment of the National Capital which has already a general conception of its direction for future growth. The purpose of the study was to guide students skilled in other fields of design to utilize the fundamentals of city planning in dealing with physical environment at a large scale.

unique opportunity for a rich program of advanced study and research and for collaborating with other Departments at the Institute in new approaches to urban and metropolitan growth. The focus of teaching was described as lying neither in design nor in economic or social studies *per se,* but centering on the "man-made *physical* environment on the large scale of cities or regions; how it can be manipulated; and its causes or consequences: technical, aesthetic, social, and psychological."

To enlist support for a new program, an *ad hoc* advisory committee was appointed by President Killian. Its members were Carl Feiss, Joseph L. Fisher, T. J. Kent, Jr., Arthur D. McVoy, Clarence S. Stein, and Edwin S. Burdell (Chairman). The committee's report (1956) strongly recommended the following:

LAND CHARACTER
l e g e n d
0 2 4 6m
generally flat : below 50'
"   " : 50' & above
"   rolling : directionless
major stream valleys

that a Center for Urban and Regional Studies be established within the Institute;

that a doctoral program be established in the Department of City and Regional Planning as an essential part of the mission of the Center;

that the financing of the Center be assured for at least a ten-year period;

that the Department of City Planning and Regional Studies remain under strong leadership in the School of Architecture and City Planning and continue to operate the Master of City Planning program, register doctoral candidates, and supply to the Center faculty specialists, especially in physical planning and civic design, to aid in research and in supervision of doctoral studies;

that appropriate departments in the School of Humanities and Social Studies likewise supply the Center with specialists in the social sciences and their applied fields such as public administration, education, recreation, and welfare.

The proposal for a program at the doctoral level was adopted by the Institute in 1956 when it agreed to accept candidates who studied in both the Department of City and Regional Planning and in the Department of Economics for the Ph.D. degree in planning and economics. Later, in 1958, the Institute gave final approval to the Department of City and Regional Planning to grant the Ph.D.

The recommendation of the *ad hoc* committee for the creation of a Center for Urban and Regional Studies was adopted by M.I.T. in the fall of 1957. Professor Rodwin was appointed director, and staff aid was drawn from other faculty members and graduate students whose research might be of value to the Center. The major fields of concentration were initially transportation, housing, underdeveloped areas, and the application of mathematical techniques to urban problems.

Although only one solution appears, the entire group was obliged to compress all the complex and inter-related elements of the Washington metropolitan region into relatively small diagrams. The aim of providing real diversity and unique character in a large community was of necessity an intricate and enormous process dependent upon matters of scattering, infilling, migration, and remodelling which could be encompassed but inadequately within the allotted span of time.

Population in the area was estimated to expand to 750,000 by the year 2000. Employment, transportation systems, standards of living, and leisure time were all projected in terms of future changes that are imperfectly comprehended at the present moment. A general pattern was attempted for the metropolitan sector that would appear well differentiated and well structured in all its component parts yet achieve a visual form congruent with patterns of activity that make up a human community.

PENINSULAR DEVELOPMENT

ROBERT GOODMAN

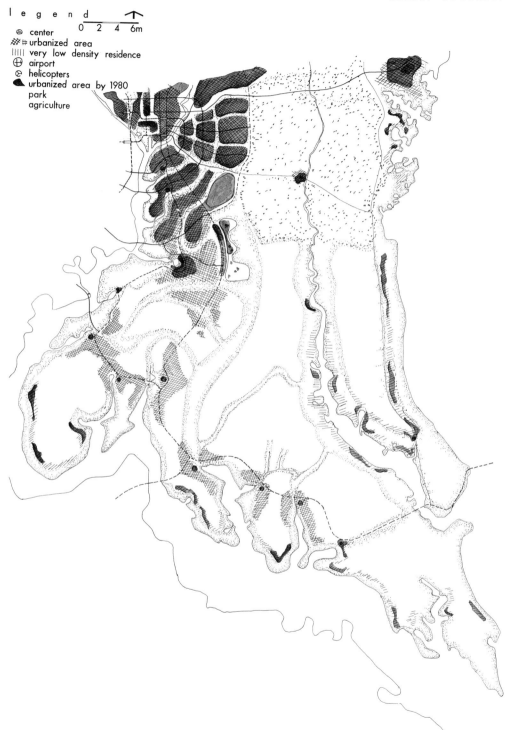

legend

0 2 4 6m

⊚ center
✷⊞ urbanized area
‖‖‖ very low density residence
⊕ airport
℗ helicopters
◣ urbanized area by 1980
park
agriculture

The resultant plans were intended as entities with emphasis on visual considerations because the latter are so often neglected in planning work. The environment was arranged to provide distinguishable parts, yet a coherent whole, capable of producing a sharp mental image. Reliance on topography and on circulation systems was unduly high, a fact which in conclusion indicated the need for emphasizing other patterns of form.

SECTOR LAND USE

ROBERT GOODMAN

101

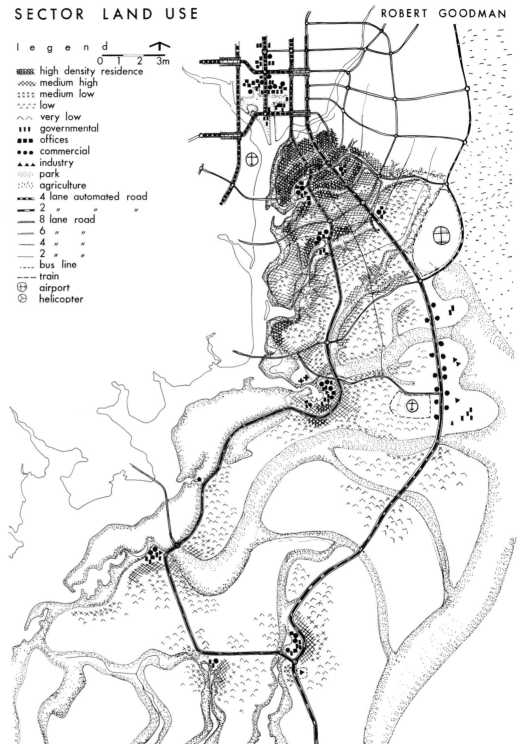

legend

0 1 2 3m

high density residence
medium high
medium low
low
very low
governmental
offices
commercial
industry
park
agriculture
4 lane automated road
2 " " "
8 lane road
6 " "
4 " "
2 " "
bus line
train
airport
helicopter

Professor Adams retired in 1957 as head of the Department of City and Regional Planning in order to devote full time to teaching. He was succeeded by John T. Howard, a member of the faculty and one of its early graduates (M.C.P., 1936). Professor Howard had also joined with Professors Adams and Greeley in forming the firm of Adams, Howard, and Greeley, planning consultants whose assignments on planning projects have ranged from New England to India. Prior to coming to the Institute, he had spent seven years as Director of the Cleveland City Planning Commission and served as adviser to the National Capital Regional Planning Council on the development of metropolitan Washington.

Research in planning was made possible by the Federal Reserve Bank in Boston, the Sears Foundation, and the Rockefeller Foundation. The first study financed by the Bank was a survey of community costs published as a book in 1957 by Professor Walter Isard and a graduate student, Robert E. Coughlin: *Municipal Costs and Revenues Resulting From Community Growth*. Professors Lynch and Kepes received a two-year grant from the Rockefeller Foundation to study the perceptual form of the city. Preliminary findings have appeared in Kevin A. Lynch's *The Image of the City,* published by the Joint Center for Urban Studies (described below) in 1960. Another study, commissioned by the American Council to Improve our Neighborhoods, was made under the direction of Professor Kelly and resulted in the book, *Design and the Production of Houses.*[67]

In April, 1959, financed by a grant from the Ford Foundation, M.I.T. and Harvard University established a Joint Center for Urban Studies to support advanced research and to stimulate interuniversity efforts in the urban field. Direction of the Center is divided equally between the Institute and Harvard. The Center has undertaken a long list of studies that relate to urban life. In addition to Professor Lynch's *The Image of the City,* it has published (1961) *Housing and Economic Progress: A Study of the Housing Experience of Boston's Middle-Income Families,* by Lloyd Rodwin, who is chairman of the Center's Faculty Committee, and a number of political and planning studies.

The proposed development of the southeast sector of Washington accepted the future metropolis as a complex, yet interconnected, dynamic form. Continuous change, with all its various drives, was part of the thesis that made flexibility one of the fundamental criteria. The methods of controlling the entire metropolitan visual form, and the implementation of the plans could not be investigated in detail on account of limitations not only of time in the curriculum but of available knowledge. Similar limitations also forced concentration on physical character and dominant visual spaces experienced as units by people moving about on main lines of circulation or within main centers of activity.

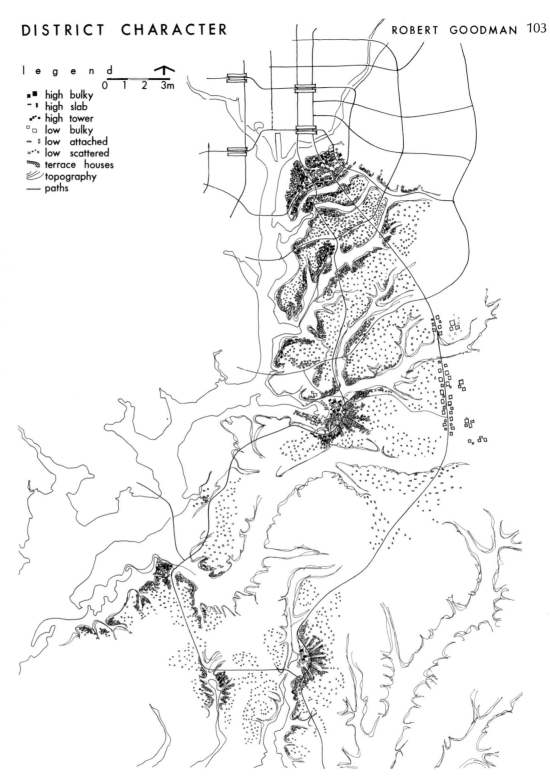

legend

- ▪■ high bulky
- ‒ı high slab
- ⟋▪⟍ high tower
- ▫▫ low bulky
- ▬ ▯ low attached
- ▫•▫•▫ low scattered
- terrace houses
- topography
- paths

0 1 2 3m

104 Difficulties were encountered in predicting, in an abstract form, the final image of the metropolitan sector. But, in discovering and recognizing these difficulties, professional development was forwarded and provocative questions raised. Momentary cross sections of a process, it was learned, could not adequately serve to delineate future patterns; moving diagrams of a kind not yet invented would be required to portray adequately the rate and shape of change and growth.

The National Capital Planning Commission sponsored the project although it was exploratory and carried out by students and staff.

DOMINANT SPACES
AND VISIBLE ACTIVITY

ROBERT GOODMAN

legend
0 1 2 3m
⌐-⌐dominant space
⫻ ⫶ visible activity

Graduates and faculty members in the Department of City and Regional Planning continued to assume significant roles in their profession. By 1961, six graduates were directors of major planning commissions in the United States. Several had joined or founded their own firms as planning consultants with world-wide commitments. Official posts in The American Institute of Planners, including the presidency, were held repeatedly by M.I.T. alumni. The Department, with twelve other schools, was co-founder of the Association of Collegiate Schools of Planning.

Schools of planning at many universities have recently been administered by M.I.T. graduates: John A. Parker '31 at the University of North Carolina, John T. Howard '35 at M.I.T., Louis B. Wetmore '36 at the University of Illinois, Thomas J. Kent, Jr. '43 at the University of California in Berkeley, Israel Stollman '48 at the Ohio State University, Carl Feiss '38 at Columbia University, and Gordon Stephenson '38 at the University of Toronto. Thomas W. Mackesey '32

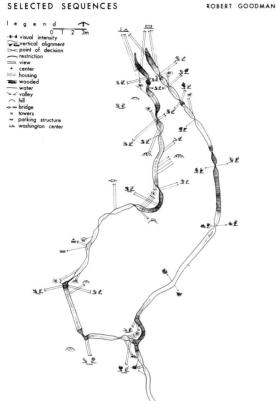

legend
- visual intensity
- vertical alignment
- point of decision
- restriction
- view
- center
- housing
- wooded
- water
- valley
- hill
- bridge
- towers
- parking structure
- washington center

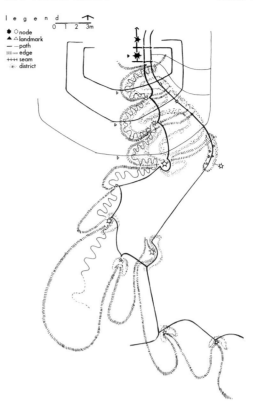

legend
- ● ○ node
- ▲ △ landmark
- — — path
- ||||||||| edge
- ++++ seam
- district

was dean of the College of Architecture at Cornell University from 1950 until 1960, when he was succeeded there by Burnham Kelly '41. Edwin S. Burdell '20, whose committee contributed constructive advice in reorganizing M.I.T.'s planning course, also taught sociology in city planning at M.I.T. from 1934 to 1938. For one year he was dean of the M.I.T. School of Humanities, and then he became president of Cooper Union in New York City.

Members of the planning faculty, like those in the Department of Architecture, were expanding their horizons through foreign study. Kevin Lynch was a Fulbright Scholar in Italy, and Lloyd Rodwin spent a year at the University of Liverpool, where his study of new towns in Great Britain resulted in a book on the subject.[68] The Department was continuing to expose its students to the divergent philosophies of contemporary thinkers such as Lewis Mumford, Albert Mayer, and others, who came to Cambridge as visiting lecturers.

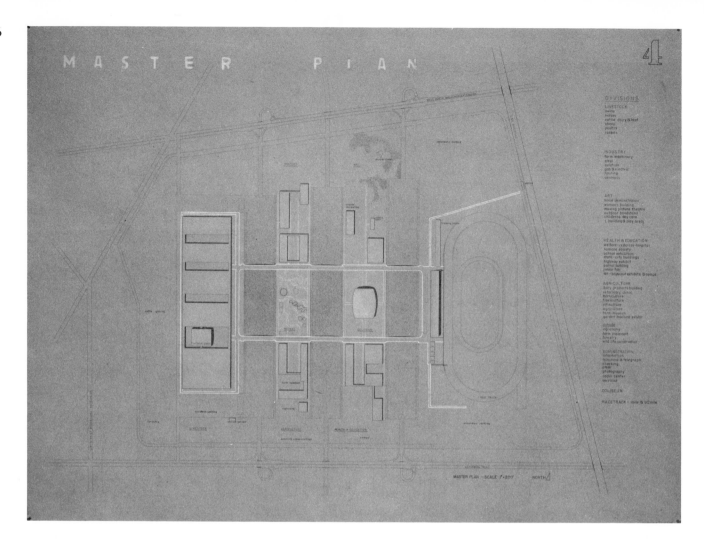

Developments in the Department of Architecture in 1949 and 1950 were based on a new approach that involved more rigorous association of students in the teaching process. Team work was encouraged in preparing solutions to problems, so that cooperation began to replace individual competition. To aid in developing an understanding and total picture of the many facets of architecture, "live" problems were given as often as possible. Clients, site, soil conditions, technical requirements, and esthetic demands were made as real as possible so that students would learn to think through actual, rather than artificial, situations. Professor Anderson assembled a staff composed of a core of senior critics assisted by young instructors. Acting as a jury, the staff was able to hold effective public discussions and criticisms of student work. Professor Anderson also supplemented design problems with series of sketch problems to improve skill in graphic presentation. He brought reality into the curriculum by initiating a course on the industrialized house, a broad study of mass housing and its production, distribution, financing, and social factors.

A conference on the same subject, sponsored by the Bemis Foundation in January, 1951, attracted participants from various segments of industry and government and brought large-scale building problems into the course of study. The conclusions of the conference were published under the title, *Housing, A National Security Resource.* Earlier, in 1950, the Foundation had published its survey, *Social Pressures in Informal Groups, A Study of Human Factors in Housing,* by Leon Festinger, Stanley Schacter, and Kurt Back. The book was a major study resulting from an investigation of the psychological factors affecting the mass production of houses. Beginning in 1951-1952, an annual fellowship in housing administered by the Foundation was established to enable a graduate student to pursue research in the wide range of fields pertaining to housing.

Papers from the Bemis Foundation conference in 1952, to explore the application of mass production to the house-building industry, were later published under the title:

The American fair developed primarily as a means of exchanging information on farming, livestock, and homemaking; but as media of communication improved, fairs increased in size and altered in character. The trend was toward more entertainment, professional exhibits, and junior activities. Ample, permanent buildings were required, such as those designed by Thomas F. McNulty for his Master's thesis, A New Ohio State Fair, 1949.

Housing—Mass-Produced. The conference subject in the following year was economic development and housing abroad, an exploration of the role of architects and community planners in the foreign economic programs of the United States.[69]

Buckminster Fuller, appointed visiting critic for a number of years, provoked imaginative thinking in adapting structural techniques to enclose space for dwellings or other purposes. Conventional building, as he pointed out, involves wasteful methods. In order to stimulate discovery of completely new processes, Fuller, in lectures and criticisms, ranged over large areas of knowledge. He sought always, at M.I.T. and elsewhere, to open new channels of thought, to explore with his students new approaches to the entire building field, and to encourage practical experimentation. The Acoustics Laboratory at M.I.T. was tapped as a logical area of research for architects, especially in the fifth-year and graduate class, where the behavior of sound could be examined in relation to enclosed space. Robert B. Newman (M. Arch., 1949), who now teaches in the School, has become one of the nation's leading authorities on architectural acoustics. As vice president of Bolt, Beranek, and Newman, he has collaborated in the design of more than five hundred buildings in the United States and overseas.

Since 1948 an exchange of teachers with foreign universities has been an invigorating experience for the School. The Royal Academy of Fine Arts in Copenhagen has sent several members of its faculty—practicing architects of distinction, including Kay Fisker and Steen Eiler Rasmussen—to the United States; and several M.I.T. faculty, including Professor Anderson, have gone to teach a year at the Royal Academy.

For M.I.T., as for the country and the international scene as well, the mid-point of the twentieth century saw realization of several forces which had been emerging for the past fifty years. One marked change was the shift in geographic focus of building activity. No longer was it concentrated wholly in the major European countries; the United States, Latin America, Scandinavia, and other nations of

A Civic Theater and Auditorium for the City of Indianapolis, Indiana, by Donald E. Clark, 1950. Seating capacity of the main auditorium was 13,000, the music hall 3,000, and the small auditorium 500.

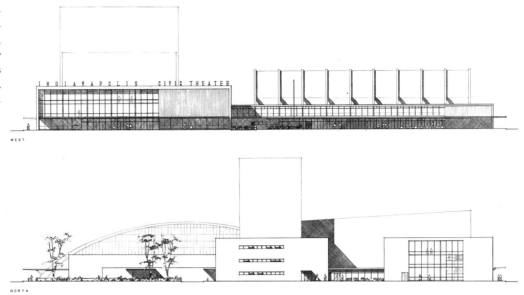

WEST

NORTH

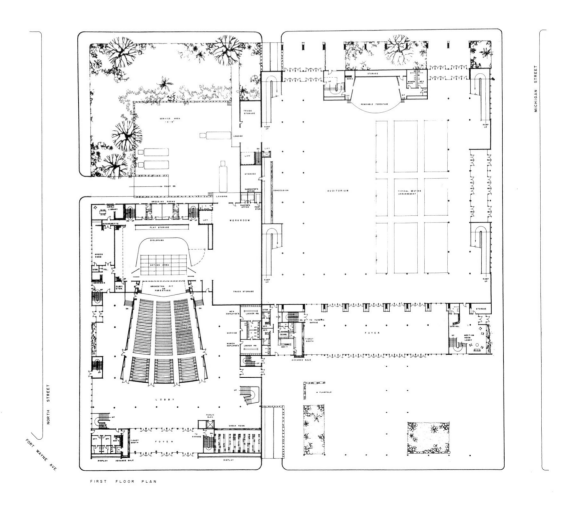

FIRST FLOOR PLAN

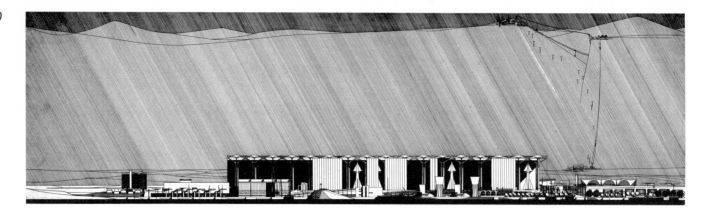

Jacques Binoux's Master's thesis, 1957, was A Study in Design of Ground Facilities for Launching and Landing of Space Ships. Undaunted by the engineering problems involved, Binoux chose a site on Martinique Island in the Antilles for a stratoport that would deliver passengers and cargo to a space station 1075 miles above the earth.

the world were developing new and individual forms. Another trend was a sophisticated adaptation of technology to design; architecture had become a unified process that could utilize structural elements and materials to satisfy esthetic demands.

Wurster left M.I.T. in 1950 to become dean of the College of Architecture at the University of California, and the man chosen by M.I.T. to take his place was a man of the new era, Pietro Belluschi. He regarded architecture in its broad, universal context as "creating the kind of environment where different minds and talents may find stimulus, motivation, and a sense of direction."[70]

Pietro Belluschi was born in Italy and educated at the University of Rome, where he received a Doctor of Architectural Engineering degree. He came to the United States to study at Cornell University and since then has received honorary degrees from other colleges. Moving to Oregon, he designed many distinguished structures, including the Equitable Savings and Loan Building in Portland, one of the first post-war skyscrapers to reveal its structural outline interspaced with windows of colored glass and spandrels of aluminum. Other notable buildings among Dean Belluschi's works are the First Presbyterian Church, Cottage Grove, Oregon; the Church of the Redeemer, Baltimore; the First Lutheran Church of Boston; the Chapel, Portsmouth Priory, Rhode Island; and the Pan American Building, New York City. He has been involved in many ways in determining the trend of building both here and abroad, in an advisory capacity to the State Department and through his own private work. Recognition of his leadership in the fine arts has come from many sources, including membership in the American Academy of Arts and Sciences and the National Institute of Arts and Letters.

A basic policy of the School in educating its students for their role in a changing and ever-broadening society was defined in Dean Belluschi's annual report for 1954-55, when he proposed to invite "outstanding, even controversial, personalities in architecture or the arts and men of worldwide repute" to teach or lecture at M.I.T. This policy has not been limited to single individuals but has been expanded to groups of professionals and government officials who have been invited to participate in conferences and symposia. To sum up Pietro Belluschi's philosophy of education:

The aim of our School is not to produce a sort of professional man in quantity, but rather to make it possible for each student to become an architect of individual quality.[71]

Private practice by members of its teaching staff is encouraged by the School, in the belief that this will tend to prevent the faculty from falling into sterile academic ways of thought. Thus a live, realistic climate has been created throughout the School.

Research, as part of the educational process, is encouraged so that the School is able to explore climate,[72] acoustics, illumination, prefabrication, and other technical problems of the building industry. Material aid continues to come from the Bemis Foundation and from other sources, including Wakefield Brass Company and Reynolds Aluminum Company. Through repeated grants-in-aid from the Monsanto Chemical Company, experiments in plastics as building materials have been undertaken to explore their application to the industrial production of both houses[73] and schools.[74] An all-plastic house, designed and constructed under the direction of Professor Marvin E. Goody, has found its way to Disneyland in California, where it is part of the permanent exhibition of the future aspect of America. In 1955 M.I.T. won four prizes, including the first prize, in a competition sponsored by the Society of Plastic Industries. The project for the year 1961-62 was the actual construction on the campus of a schoolhouse of prefabricated panels. The construction and design of the prototype was sponsored by the Educational Facilities Laboratory, Inc., of New York. The project was developed jointly by the Departments of Architecture and of Civil Engineering, with cooperation from twenty major companies in the building materials industry.

In the year 1952-53 enrollment increased to the largest in the history of the School, 193 students. A new course

The design by David Ernest Horne for the Toronto City Hall and Square was one of eight out of 519 entries chosen for the final stage of the competition. It was agreed that the final presentation (appearing on this and the following page) would become Horne's thesis for his Master in Architecture in 1958.

in visual design was directed by Richard Filipowski to develop a sense of three-dimensional awareness. Through actual construction of small objects from various materials, students are led to think in three-dimensional terms and to understand the interrelationships of forms and space. Freshman drawing, however, was not dropped from the curriculum, and good draftsmanship is actually receiving greater emphasis than it has for the past twenty years. The use of architectural materials in a studio provides a more vivid experience than renderings in one flat dimension, no matter how well executed. Inventive thinking and creativity are fostered by teamwork on projects, open discussion of problems, and participation in research on the use of materials. With the introduction, also, of the element of color, spatial perception becomes more acute. Photographic studies, directed by Professor Kepes,[75] sharpen visual awareness not only of individual architectural concepts but also of total environment.

When the new Hayden Library was built, adequate gallery space for art exhibits first became available at M.I.T. Under the direction of Professor Beckwith as chairman of the Technology Museum Committee, exhibitions of contemporary painting and sculpture occur at regular intervals throughout the year, and there are annual teaching shows of Greek and Renaissance art.

The point-of-view of the student and his responsibilities toward the profession of architecture were stated in a booklet written and edited in 1955 by five members of the class. "Good architecture," they declare in the introduction, "can be nothing short of the best provision for meeting contemporary requirements." *Architecture, Theory and Craftsmanship*[76] supports through text and illustrations its central theme that skilled craftsmanship, combined with theoretical understanding, can create "an architecture that satisfies the needs and expresses the highest aims of our civilization."[77] In eleven chapters, ranging from an evaluation of the Katsura Palace to an article on political expression in architecture, the booklet presents enthusiastic and thoughtful comments on the best ways of solving contemporary problems.

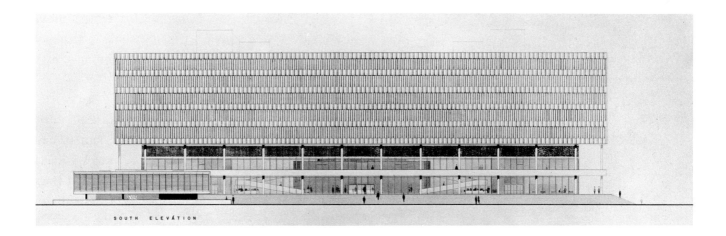

SOUTH ELEVATION

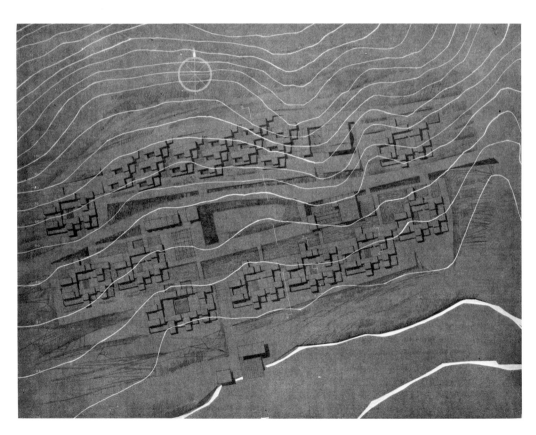

A Housing Development for Greece: Design for a Community on Mount Kojakas, by Alexis Papageorgiou, 1958. In describing this project for his Master's thesis, Papageorgiou wrote, *The proposed community is one of approximately seventy families whose breadwinners will be working in a mountainous and pine-forested region in Greece. The site is on the steep south slope of Mount Kojakas in the Province of Trikala. The ground is rocky. The summer is long, and yet occasional light snow is encountered in winter.*

Economy and tradition have been major influences on the design proposals for both the community as a whole and for the houses. Economy dic- *tates, among other things, the use of concrete. The planning is intended to re-create traditional concepts in contemporary spatial forms.*

The core of the community runs along the contour through the center. A sunken "Gymnasium" is flanked by two Agoras; these latter symbolise the two centers of human exchange — the exchange of ideas and the exchange of goods — a concept expressed in the writings of Aristotle and in the city planning of ancient Greece. The church or "Temple" is set on slightly higher ground, so that the symbol of the sublime visually dominates the community.

Houses are combined and related to each other in two *forms. The more complex form, on the lower part of the slope, is explored in detail in this thesis. These houses are grouped into clusters accommodating six families. Each cluster has a central Atrium, and each house has a private, smaller Atrium. Orientation is to the desirable southeast, while north and west walls are of unbroken character. Lightweight concrete shells are a feature in the simple and modular planning and structure, which is generally governed by the overall demand for economy.*

The design provides for and symbolizes that strong sense of local community that has traditionally inspired Greek city form.

118

Theodore John Musho chose Columbus Circle in New York City for the site of his Master's thesis, A Catholic Information Center, 1959. Locating his church at a growing center of the city, where it could stand physically free from its surroundings, Musho intended his design to be strong enough to create "a visual perimeter for the Circle, hoping thereby that the parts of the perimeter will create a sequence of related events that amplify the civic character of the Columbus and Maine monuments."

Throughout his administration, Dean Belluschi has sought to encourage respect for facts and to inculcate an understanding of techniques. Teamwork by students in coordinating results and expressing them in clear and creative designs stimulates effective thinking and helps each student acquire a sense of standards. Motivation, creative ability, and wisdom can be developed through knowledge and discipline. This has been the ideal upon which teaching is based.

The wide horizon of current architecture and building is brought each year within the students' scope of awareness by visiting lecturers and critics. Architects from foreign countries—Sven Markelius from Sweden, Steen Eiler Rasmussen from Denmark, Kenzo Tange from Japan, and many others—have brought the breadth of their experience into the classroom in juries and seminars. Jane Drew, British architect whose work virtually extends around the globe from England to Pakistan, West Africa, and India, gave instruction for one term in building in the hot-dry and hot-humid countries of the world.

In the summer of 1960, ten students and three faculty members made a six-week tour of South America, primarily of Chile, under the sponsorship of the State Department as part of the International Educational Exchange Program. The group was returning a visit paid to the United States by Chilean architecture students in 1959.

To improve the effectiveness of its teaching program, the Department of Architecture has continued to add to its ranks architects with diverse backgrounds. Eduardo Catalano, who joined the staff in 1956, had an active career as a practicing architect in Buenos Aires from 1941 to 1950 and had taught in London, at North Carolina State College, and at the University of Buenos Aires. He received a Master of Architecture degree from Harvard University and was acting head of the Department of Architecture in the School of Design at North Carolina State College when called to M.I.T. Professor Catalano's structural use of the hyperbolic paraboloid in his own house in Raleigh, North Carolina, has received world-wide attention for its spectacular appearance and its technical value in proving that

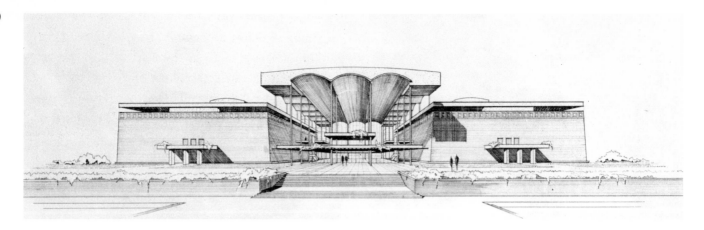

A Capitol for the Republic of Korea, by Ki Suh Park, 1959, was designed to replace the building destroyed during the Korean War. Park's scheme, presented in a Master's thesis, was proposed to harmonize with an ancient palace of the kings that was unique in construction and a source of inspiration to the people of Korea.

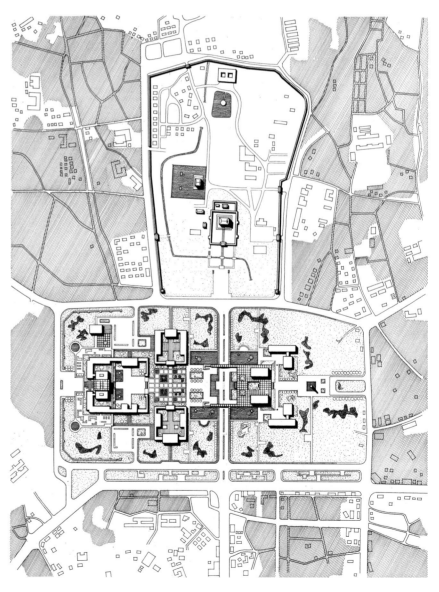

a single warped plane could span a roof of a one-story 121
building of almost any size without the support of columns.

Imre Halasz came to the School from the University of Budapest to teach advanced design. His strong European view of the cultural significance of architecture, emphasized in his teaching, tends to produce a thoughtful approach to the solution of problems. Since 1956 Joseph Hudnut, former Dean of the Harvard Graduate School of Design, has given an elective course on the structure of the city, the objective of which is to develop independent judgment of the urban scene. Professor Hudnut has donated his entire personal collection of several thousand slides to the library.

In 1956 the program in visual arts was recognized by the Institute as a field of elective study to fulfill humanities requirements of students in the Schools of Engineering, Industrial Management, and Science. Designated as Field 10 of the humanities electives, the program is directed by Professors Albert Bush-Brown and Robert Preusser. It includes lectures in history and criticism of art, seminars, and studio work.

Summer seminars for teachers and interested members of other professions have also been offered in the field of visual arts. The first, conducted in 1954 by Professor Filipowski, dealt with design fundamentals—the interrelations between light, color, shapes, and volumes. This was followed by seminars on other architectural subjects in succeeding summers.

Student achievements have been recognized both here and abroad. Thymio Papayannis '57 of Greece was chiefly responsible for organizing the National Association of Students of Architecture under the aegis of the American Institute of Architects, a long-needed activity. For his endeavors Papayannis was elected first president of the Association. Two years after his graduation Papayannis won a national competition in Greece for a National Railroads Office Building in Athens that has now been constructed. A thesis entitled *A Stratoport,* written by Jacques Binoux, Grunsfeld Fellow from France, received the Thesis Award for 1957 from the National Institute for Architectural Education.

In the 1958 international competition for a City Hall in Toronto, David Horne, a graduate student, was one among eight who passed the first stage and was invited to submit final designs from which the winning architect would be chosen. The eight finalists included two alumni of M.I.T., Ieoh M. Pei '40 and William B. Hayward '55.

From Italy came an unexpected award in 1960 when the Grand International Prize, la Rinascente Compasso d'Oro, was bestowed upon the School. Although the Prize is intended to honor achievement specifically in industrial design, it was conferred in appreciation of the courses in visual design directed by Professor Kepes since 1946.

Two new traveling scholarships have been donated, one by Skidmore, Owings and Merrill, the other by Ernest A. Grunsfeld, Jr.[78] of the Class of 1918. Fulbright Scholarships are awarded rather generously to M.I.T., allowing as many as eight students to travel in foreign countries in one year. An American Academy in Rome Fellowship was awarded to Theodore J. Musho in 1959. The Rotch Traveling Scholarship was won in 1961 by Joseph O. Cotton '59 with Kay M. Lockhart '60 as alternate, thus bringing to thirty-five the number of winners who had attended or graduated from M.I.T. William E. Hartmann '37 has established a scholarship which will bear his name and become available in 1962 to assist students who hold degrees from an institution not offering professional architectural studies.

In 1948 Henry-Russell Hitchcock[79] wrote that "today's students will probably not be carrying out their most important work until the 1960's and 1970's." What image passed across his mind? Did he visualize an embassy in Ghana, Lever House in New York City, or the Mile High Center in Denver? Did he see a new town in Israel, a housing project in Chicago, or urban renewal in Boston? Did he visualize the Earth Sciences Building (now under construction) conceived for M.I.T. by one of its own alumni?

The art of building was changing rapidly. For M.I.T.'s centenary[80] in 1961 the Department of Architecture prepared a retrospective exhibit of American architecture that was a graphic review of the past hundred years in

A Prototype Floor Structure, by Bruce E. Erickson, 1960, was an investigation of reinforced concrete in producing a floor system.

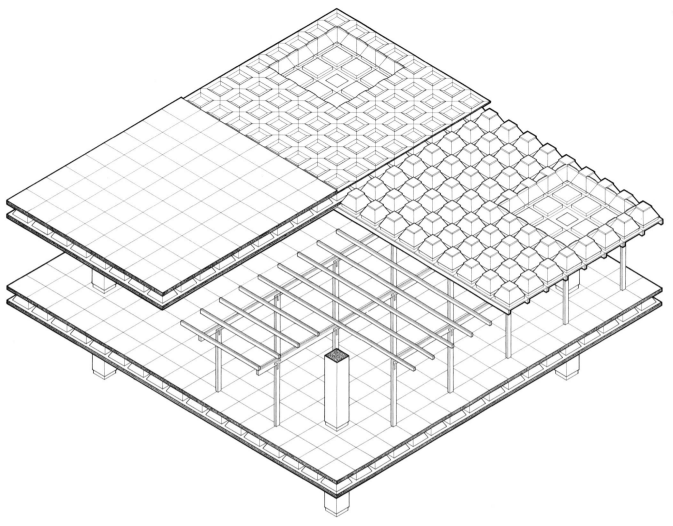

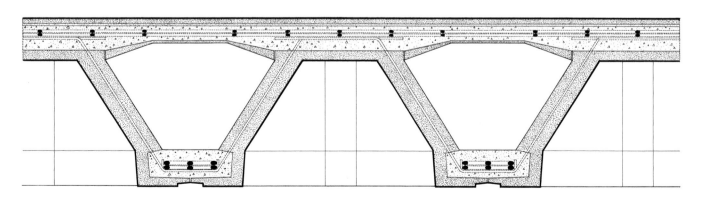

DIAGONAL SECTION
SCALE: 1-1/2" = 1'-0"

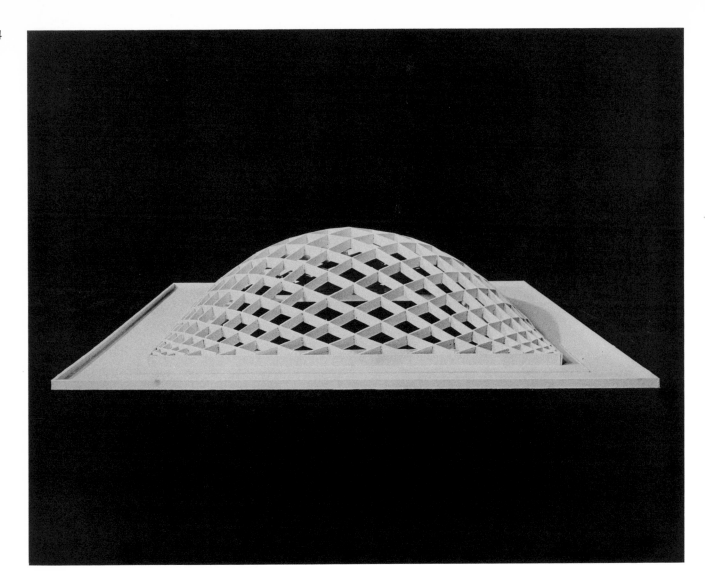

An Air Inflated Structure, by Richard Baker Morrill and Kay Milton Lockhart, 1960, is shown in this photograph of the model. With relatively little research being done outside of specialized functions for the Army and Air Force, the authors collaborated in a project to investigate the structural and architectural implications of air structures. The following paragraph is quoted from their abstract:

Brief investigation into the air structure concept has been motivated by an interest in the potential of new flexible materials to create long spans when the material is made rigid through air pressure. This economy of material for certain span conditions seems appealing, and with the proper technology perhaps could result in low-cost structures for various uses.

building design and construction. Recent technological developments were portrayed in the exploitation of metals under tension that have already resulted in the Unistrut and geodesic dome type of structure and in reinforced concrete, indicating potentialities of form not yet played out in architectural imagination.

In an age of rapid technological development, bursting populations, expanding industrialization, and urbanization of once primitive communities, the future of education for young men who aspire to become architects and city planners raises many questions. The School must critically and continually examine its curriculum, study its methods, and review its role in forming man's physical environment in order "to promote more effective professional action."

In the introduction to its latest booklet, the School states its objectives:

Architecture and city planning, though distinct professions with separate problems and tools, are ultimately concerned with a single objective: creating a more civilized physical environment. It is increasingly clear that the aims of architecture and city planning will be most fully realized through collaboration between the two disciplines, bringing design skills to bear on the relationships of buildings to each other, to the land, and to other elements of the urban structure. The need and the opportunity are now greater than ever before: we are entering an era of large-scale city development projects—urban renewal, industrial parks, government centers, new suburbs, and central business building groups.[81]

The pioneering in education that began one hundred years ago continues with undiminished vigor.

1   W. B. Rogers, *Life and Letters* (Boston: Houghton, Mifflin and Company, 1896) I, p. 261.

2   Ware lived from 1832 to 1915.

3   M.I.T. Archives. Letter from W. R. Ware, Apr. 27, 1865.

4   W. R. Ware, "On the Condition of Architecture and of Architectural Education in the United States," *Sessional Papers of the Royal Institute of British Architects* (London, 1867), pp. 85-86: *"We have at the present moment no system of professional education, young men educating themselves, and picking up in offices what they may, some as pupils and some as draughtsmen, of whom the latter are rather the best off, as it is important to their employers that they should know something, while the pupils, who sometimes pay fees and sometimes not, are left pretty much to their own devices.*

"The only scheme of education which has existed within my own experience, other than this desultory work in offices, was established by Mr. Richard Hunt, whose name I have mentioned, and who, after his return from Paris, opened in New York an atelier, upon the French system, and for four or five years had a small class of students who enthusiastically pursued, under his electric influence, the study of architectural drawing and composition. A mere private establishment of this sort, dependent upon the energy and devotion of one man, suffered, of course,

from the lack of the regulating and sustaining influence which the Ecole des Beaux-Arts exerts upon the ateliers which supplement it; and Mr. Hunt's élèves were, of course, utterly without the systematic instruction by lectures in history, science, and construction, which, to a certain extent, supply in Paris the deficiencies of mere atelier education. But he was able to breathe into it what was more important than all this—the atmosphere of the Paris school; and his studio, while it lasted, was a real home of art , a real fountain of inspiration. From this school were recruited many of the younger members of the Institute, who, joining it as Associates, sat at the feet of their elders during their noviciate and have since ascended to the upper seats."

5   M.I.T. Archives. Letter from W. R. Ware, Apr. 27, 1865.

6   W. R. Ware, "On the Condition of Architecture," pp. 81-82.

7   J. B. A. Lassus, *Album de Villard de Honnecourt, Architecte du XIIIᵉ Siècle.* A. Darcel (ed.). Manuscrit publié en fac-simile. (Paris: Imprimerie Imperiale, 1858).

8   Palladio and Vignola were close students of Vitruvius.

9   J. Androuet du Cerceau, Jacques François Blondel, etc.

10 Philibert de l'Orme; Jean Bullant, and others.

11 W. R. Ware, *An Outline of a Course in Architectural Instruction* (Boston: Press of John Wilson and Sons, 1866). Reprinted by the F. W. Boles Memorial Fund, 1942.

12 W. R. Ware, "On the Condition of Architecture," p. 86.

13 M.I.T. Archives. Letter from W. R. Ware, Apr. 27, 1865.

14 W. R. Ware, *An Outline of a Course,* p. 29.

15 M.I.T. Archives. Letter from T. M. Clark, Oct. 3, 1881.

16 Massachusetts Institute of Technology. *President's Report for the Year Ending Sept. 30, 1875,* pp. 148-149.

17 Text on a plaque in Building 7, M.I.T., Cambridge: *"Eugène Létang (1842-1892). Born at Boulleret, France, in the Province of Berri. He came to Boston in 1871. For twenty-two years he taught architectural design at the Massachusetts Institute of Technology.*

In grateful memory of this loyal and fruitful service this tablet is 129
erected by his pupils and friends."

18   Massachusetts Institute of Technology. *President's Report for the Year Ending Sept. 30, 1873, p. X.*

19   *Ibid.,* p. X.

20   W. R. Ware, *Modern Perspective: A Treatise Upon the Principles and Practice of Plane and Cylindrical Perspective* (Boston: J. R. Osgood and Company, 1883); text and atlas; text reprinted 1885. —, *The American Vignola.* (Boston: The American Architect and Building News Co., 1902-06). 2 vols.; also several later editions. *Shades and Shadows, With Applications to Architectural Details, and Exercises in Drawing Them With the Brush or Pen* (Scranton: International Textbook Company, 1912-13); 2 vols.

21   W. P. P. Longfellow, *Applied Perspective, for Architects and Painters* (Boston: Houghton, Mifflin and Company, 1901).

22   W. P. P. Longfellow, *Column and the Arch. Essays on Architectural History* (New York: Charles Scribner's Sons, 1899). —, editor. *A Cyclopaedia of Works of Architecture in Italy, Greece, and the Levant* (New York: Charles Scribner's Sons, 1895).

23   R. Turner, *On the Use of Water Colors for Beginners* (Boston: Prang, 1886).

24   D. A. Gregg, *Architectural Rendering in Pen and Ink* (Chicago: American School of Correspondence, 1903).

25   Clark was the author of two books: *Building Superintendence, a Manual for Young Architects, Students, and Others Interested in Building Operations as Carried on at the Present Day* (Boston: J. R. Osgood & Company, 1885); and *Architect, Owner and Builder Before the Law* (New York: Macmillan and Co., 1894).

26   C. H. Blackall, *Envois of the Rotch Travelling Scholarship, a Selection of European Notes and Sketches Taken From the Work of the First and Second Holders of the Rotch Travelling Scholarships, Boston, Massachusetts* (New York: for sale by S. M. O'Neill, 188?). Boston Society of Architects. *Envois of the Rotch Travelling Scholarship 1885-1892* (1896).

       C. H. Blackall, *A History of the Rotch Travelling Scholarship 1883 to 1938* (privately printed, 1938).

27   Established in 1867.

28   Massachusetts Institute of Technology. *Annual Report of the President and Treasurer of the Massachusetts Institute of Technology,* Dec. 9, 1891, p. 38.

29   Massachusetts Institute of Technology. *Course IV. Department of Architecture* (Boston: Alfred Mudge & Son, 1890), p. 3.

30   *Ibid.,* p. 4.

31   *Ibid.,* p. 4.

32   Massachusetts Institute of Technology. *Department of Architecture. Catalogue of the Library* (Boston: Collins Press, 1892).

33   Volume 1, No. 1, Nov. 15, 1887 to Volume 3, No. 8, Dec. 31, 1890. Publication discontinued.

34   *Architects' and Builders' Magazine,* IX (1908), p. 165.

35   Massachusetts Institute of Technology. *Annual Report of the President and Treasurer,* Dec. 13, 1893, pp. 45-46.

36   Massachusetts Institute of Technology. *Annual Report of the President and Treasurer,* Dec. 12, 1894, p. 63.

37   *Ibid.,* p. 46.

38   L. H. Sullivan, *The Autobiography of an Idea* (New York: Press of the American Institute of Architects, Inc., 1926), p. 186.

39   *Ibid.,* p. 187.

40   Instruction in architecture had been offered in the courses of study prior to the establishment of the professional curriculum in 1873.

41   Manuscript in M.I.T. Archives: *"The study of Roman architecture, at least in its elements, should follow directly upon that of Greek, but at this point I believe it would be desirable if the course in architectural history could be suspended and all possible time devoted to the general survey of the later Greek world, the Roman Empire, and the transition to Byzantine and Mediaeval civilization. Thereafter the study of architectural history should be resumed and a careful presentation given of the development*

and interrelations of the Byzantine, Saracenic (or Coptic), Romanesque, and Gothic styles. Here, I am inclined to believe, the special course in the history of architecture should end. The character of Renaissance and subsequent styles should be outlined, if possible, in the general cultural course . . ."

42   Boston, 1893.

43   Boston, 1895, and later editions.

44   Boston, Bates & Guild Company, 1902.

45   Exhibits were sent also to the St. Louis Exhibition in 1904.

46   Massachusetts Institute of Technology. *Catalogue Dec., 1910* (Cambridge: 1910), p. 80.

47   Established in 1894.

48   Taylor had worked in the office of Cass Gilbert, who later achieved fame for his design of the Woolworth Building in New York City.

49   R. A. Cram, *My Life in Architecture* (Boston: Little, Brown, and Company, 1936), pp. 205-213 *passim*.

50   *Catalogue of the Premiated Drawings of the Architectural Department of the Massachusetts Institute of Technology* (Boston: Architectural Society, 1891, 1892, 1894, 1895, 1896, 1897, 1898, 1899, 1900); and *The Architectural Annual* (Boston: Architectural Society, 1900-01, 1901-02, 1902-03, 1903-04, 1904-05).

51   E. S. Campbell also became a noted painter in water color.

52   W. Emerson, "The American Students' Reconstruction Unit," *The Tech Engineering News*, II (1922), pp. 175, 181.

53   Society of Technology Architects. *Constitution and By-laws*. 1916.

54   Massachusetts Institute of Technology. *Reports of the President and Treasurer for the Year 1919-1920*, p. 53.

55   M.I.T. Archives.

56   J. Carlu, "Modernism in Architecture. New Uses for Buildings and New Building Materials Give New Fields for Creative

Ability," *The Tech Engineering News,* X (1929), pp. 223, 244.

57   Massachusetts Institute of Technology. *Bulletin. President's Report Issue 1937-1938* (Cambridge: 1938), pp. 20-23.

58   The first degree granted was the Bachelor of Architecture in City Planning authorized in 1932 and first awarded in 1935. The Institute approved the Master in City Planning degree in 1935.

59   Massachusetts Institute of Technology. *Undergraduate and Graduate Courses in City Planning* (Cambridge: 1935), p.1.

60   F. J. Adams, "The Planning Schools. I. Massachusetts Institute of Technology," *Town Planning Review,* XX (1949), pp. 144-149.

61   Presently Dean of the College of Architecture, Cornell University.

62   Massachusetts Institute of Technology. *President's Report Issue 1942-1943* (Cambridge: 1943), p. 21: *"During the past dozen years the problems of architecture and of architectural schools have been complex and difficult. It was one of the professions hardest hit by the depression. This obstacle, followed by the war, came just at the time when the 'modern' or functional architecture appeared in the field as a competitor with the more classical point of view. It is impossible to predict the exact outcome of this competition, but it is abundantly clear that the new movement is having a profound effect upon architectural thinking and practice. The trends emphasize the value of a technological environment around an architectural school."*

63   G. Kepes, *The New Landscape in Art and Science* (Chicago: Paul Theobald and Co., 1956).

64   Cranbrook Academy was founded by Eliel Saarinen.

65   Professor Rapson left M.I.T. in 1954 to become dean of the School of Architecture at the University of Minnesota.

66   Massachusetts Institute of Technology. *Solar House IV* (Cambridge: 1958).

67   B. Kelly, in association with [others], *Design and the Production of Houses* (New York: McGraw-Hill Book Company, Inc., 1959).

68   L. Rodwin, *The British New Towns Policy: Problems and Implications* (Cambridge: Harvard University Press, 1956).

69 Attention to problems of housing abroad is considered valuable   133
for the many students in the School who come to the United
States from foreign countries and would like training to prepare
them to deal with their own problems, and also for increasing
numbers of students in this country who desire to work overseas.

70 Massachusetts Institute of Technology. *The Reports of the President and of the Deans of the Schools for the Year Ending Oct. 1, 1955* (Cambridge: 1955), p. 60.

71 *Ibid.,* p. 60.

72 Results of research and studies were published by the U. S. Housing and Home Finance Agency as *Application of Climatic Data to House Design* (Washington: Government Printing Office, 1954).

   A preliminary survey by Thomas Vietorisz in 1954 had gathered together as many as possible of the technical, economic, and design considerations involved in the climate control of houses and similar small structures. The mimeographed report was distributed under the title, *Design of Residences for Climatic Comfort; A Survey of the Technical and Economic Problems Facing the Architect and the Building and Climate Control Industries.* Research by Aladar and Victor Olgyay was later made available in printed form: *Solar Control & Shading Devices* (Princeton: Princeton University Press, 1957).

73 Massachusetts Institute of Technology, Department of Architecture. *Architectural Evolution and Engineering Analysis of a Plastic House of the Future* (Cambridge: 1957); Massachusetts Institute of Technology, Department of Architecture. *Plastics in Housing* (Cambridge: 1955); and Massachusetts Institute of Technology, Department of Architecture. *Building with Plastic Structural Sandwich Panels* (Cambridge: 1958).

74 Massachusetts Institute of Technology, Department of Architecture. *Plastic Structural Sandwich Panels in an Elementary School* (Cambridge: 1959).

75 Professor Kepes received a Guggenheim Fellowship in 1961 for studies on light and color carried out at the American Academy in Rome.

76 Massachusetts Institute of Technology. *Architecture, Theory and Craftsmanship.* Designed, edited, written by students in architecture at M.I.T. (Cambridge: 1955).

134

77   *Ibid.*, Introduction.

78   The Ernest A. Grunsfeld Fund provides a sum of money for a period of travel and study in Europe for a student who would otherwise be unable to do so.

79   Massachusetts Institute of Technology, School of Architecture and Planning. *Education of Architects and City Planners* (Cambridge: 1949).

80   Massachusetts Institute of Technology. *A Century of American Building 1860-1960. A Centennial Exhibition at the Massachusetts Institute of Technology, Rogers Lobby, Building 7, 77 Massachusetts Avenue, Cambridge, April 3-30, 1961* (Cambridge: 1961).

81   Massachusetts Institute of Technology, School of Architecture and Planning. *School of Architecture and Planning. The Programs of the School; Education in Architecture; Education in Planning; Research Programs* (Cambridge: 1960).